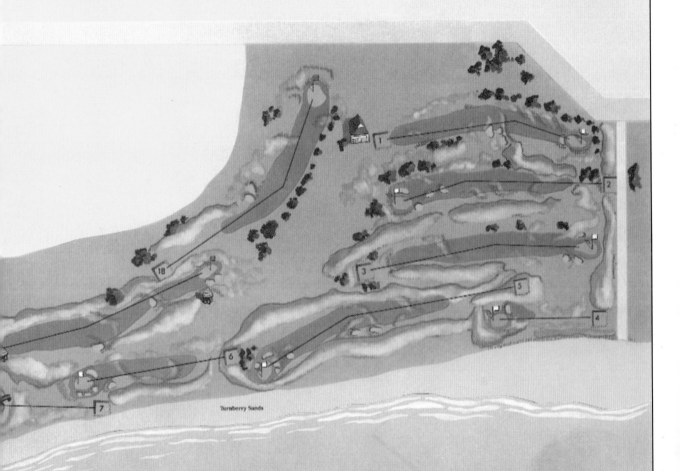

Turnberry Sands

Turnberry Bay

1994 OPEN CHAMPIONSHIP
THE AILSA COURSE, TURNBERRY
OFFICIAL CARD OF THE COURSE

Hole	Name	Yards	Par	Hole	Name	Yards	Par
1	Ailsa Craig	350	4	10	Dinna Fouter	452	4
2	Mak Siccar	428	4	11	Maidens	177	3
3	Blaw Wearie	462	4	12	Monument	448	4
4	Woe-be-Tide	167	3	13	Tickly Tap	411	4
5	Fin'me oot	441	4	14	Risk-an-Hope	440	4
6	Tappie Toorie	222	3	15	Ca Canny	209	3
7	Roon the Ben	528	5	16	Wee Burn	410	4
8	Goat Fell	430	4	17	Lang Whang	498	5
9	Bruce's Castle	452	4	18	Ailsa Hame	432	4
	Out	3480	35		In	3477	35
					Out	3480	35
					Total	6957	70

THE OPEN CHAMPIONSHIP
1994

PRESENTED IN ASSOCIATION WITH

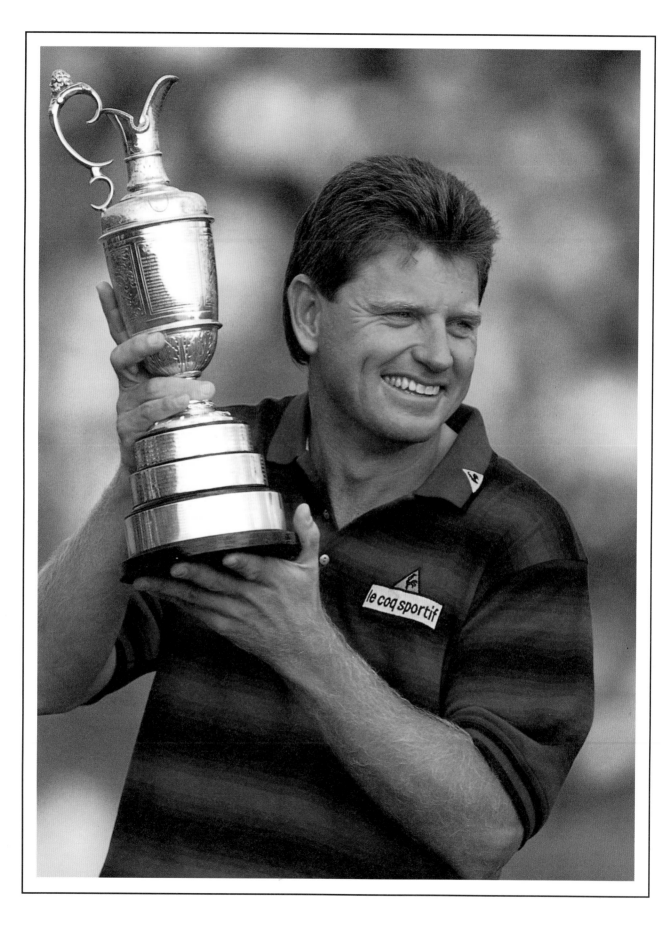

THE OPEN CHAMPIONSHIP 1994

WRITERS

ROBERT SOMMERS
RAYMOND JACOBS
MICHAEL MCDONNELL
MICHAEL WILLIAMS
MARINO PARASCENZO
ALISTER NICOL
JOHN HOPKINS

PHOTOGRAPHERS

LAWRENCE LEVY
MICHAEL COHEN
FRED VUICH

EDITOR

BEV NORWOOD

AUTHORISED BY THE
CHAMPIONSHIP COMMITTEE
OF THE ROYAL AND ANCIENT
GOLF CLUB OF ST ANDREWS

TRANSWORLD PUBLISHERS LTD
61-63 Uxbridge Road, London W5 5SA

TRANSWORLD PUBLISHERS (AUSTRALIA) PTY LTD
15-23 Helles Avenue, Moorebank, NSW 2170

TRANSWORLD PUBLISHERS (NZ) LTD
Cnr Moselle and Waipareira Aves,
Henderson, Auckland

Published 1994 by Partridge Press
a division of Transworld Publishers Ltd
Copyright © 1994 The Championship Committee Merchandising
Limited

Statistics of 123rd Open Championship produced on a
Unisys Computer System

Fred Vuich is staff photographer for GOLF Magazine (USA)
and photographs are courtesy of Times Mirror Magazines, Inc.
Photographs on pp. 14-15, 19, 21, 41 courtesy of Brian Morgan
Photographs on pp. 22, 24, 25, 55, 57, 81 (Faldo) courtesy of Allsport Photographic plc

A CIP catalogue record for this book is available
from the British Library

185225 212X

Typeset by Davis Design
Printed in Great Britain
by Bath Press Colourbooks, Glasgow

CONTENTS

JETSTREAM AIRCRAFT LIMITED
A BRITISH AEROSPACE COMPANY
SIXTY YEARS OF AVIATION EXCELLENCE

INTRODUCTION

BY R. H. EVANS, C. B. E.
Chief Executive
British Aerospace plc

Nick Price, Turnberry, the golfing public, and yes, even Jesper Parnevik share something in common — they were all "winners" at the 1994 Open Championship.

British Aerospace, itself a winner in world aerospace, was again proud to share together with our international friends and business colleagues in such a magnificent event.

We congratulate Nick Price on his win and Jesper Parnevik for taking him all the way.

British Aerospace looks forward to again enjoying the unique surroundings of St Andrews' Old Course, the home of golf, for the 124th Open Championship in 1995.

R. H. Evans, C. B. E.

THE CHAMPIONSHIP COMMITTEE

CHAIRMAN

W. G. N. ROACH

DEPUTY CHAIRMAN

P. W. J. GREENHOUGH

COMMITTEE

M. VANS AGNEW
A. BRODIE
J. E. COOK
R. M. E. DAVITT
M. C. GRINT
D. J. HARRISON
G. B. HOBART
R. H. PALMER
R. P. WHITE
R. S. WHITMORE

BUSINESS SUB-COMMITTEE CHAIRMAN

H. M. CAMPBELL

RULES SUB-COMMITTEE CHAIRMAN

J. L. S. PASQUILL

ADDITIONAL MEMBER

G. B. OVENS
COUNCIL OF NATIONAL GOLF UNIONS

SECRETARY

M. F. BONALLACK, OBE

DEPUTY SECRETARY

W. G. WILSON

CHAMPIONSHIP SECRETARY

D. HILL

ASSISTANT SECRETARY (CHAMPIONSHIPS)

D. R. WEIR

CHAMPIONSHIP ASSISTANT

A. E. FARQUHAR

INTRODUCTION

BY W. G. N. ROACH
Chairman of Championship Committee
Royal and Ancient Golf Club of St Andrews

The 123rd Open Championship started in wet conditions which, after the first day, became warm and sunny with little more than a breeze. The course was in marvellous condition, even if a little soft having been saturated with over an inch of rain in the days immediately before the Championship.

This Championship marked the 40th consecutive Open appearance of Gary Player — a remarkable achievement. Sadly neither he nor Jack Nicklaus managed to make the cut at 143.

The lead constantly changed hands and for a time Tom Watson was a possible winner, but as the end drew near it seemed certain that Jesper Parnevik, whose game was so solid, would be the first champion from Sweden until he took an uncharacteristic bogey at the last hole. Meanwhile, Nick Price had a birdie at the 16th and a great eagle at the 17th and required only a 4 at the last to win. He made no mistake.

There could be no more popular champion than Price, who paid a handsome tribute to Parnevik, for whom there was great admiration and sympathy.

The Championship Committee are grateful to Turnberry Hotel and Turnberry Golf Club for all of the help and support they gave throughout the Championship.

We also wish to acknowledge the continued support of British Aerospace in the publication of this official record and we thank the photographers and writers who have helped to record a memorable Championship within its pages.

W. G. N. Roach

FOREWORD

BY NICK PRICE

My first experience of the Open Championship was watching Tony Jacklin win at Royal Lytham and St Annes in 1969. I was watching it at my home club, Warren Hills in Harare, and I can remember clearly, his emotion after winning. However, it was not until my first Open in 1975 at Carnoustie, where as an 18-year-old amateur I saw Tom Watson win, that by experiencing that emotion firsthand did I realize how important the Open Championship was or is to any golfer.

Since that moment, there has always been a burning desire inside of me to win the Open Championship. In 1982 at Royal Troon, I played my heart out for 67 holes, and with five holes to go was convinced that I was going to win. The rest is history, and I learned a very valuable lesson! In 1988 at Lytham, I applied that lesson to the best of my ability and still did not win! In retrospect it would appear that not only was my character and game being tested, but also my patience. I realized shortly after that 1988 Open, that during a major championship, it is these qualities that are tried and tested time and time again.

This year at Turnberry, I finally managed to put everything together and when I look back and see how I played the homeward nine on the final day, I feel a sense of pride and accomplishment knowing that I drew from my past experiences and applied them well. The Open Championship has been so good to me over the years, and I hope that the emotions I showed after winning will help inspire another young golfer to enjoy playing in this great championship.

Nick Price

123RD OPEN CHAMPIONSHIP

*Denotes amateurs

NAME	SCORES				TOTAL	MONEY
Nick Price, Zimbabwe	69	66	67	66	268	£110,000
Jesper Parnevik, Sweden	68	66	68	67	269	88,000
Fuzzy Zoeller, USA	71	66	64	70	271	74,000
Anders Forsbrand, Sweden	72	71	66	64	273	50,667
Mark James, England	72	67	66	68	273	50,667
David Feherty, N. Ireland	68	69	66	70	273	50,667
Brad Faxon, USA	69	65	67	73	274	36,000
Colin Montgomerie, Scotland	72	69	65	69	275	30,000
Tom Kite, USA	71	69	66	69	275	30,000
Nick Faldo, England	75	66	70	64	275	30,000
Tom Watson, USA	68	65	69	74	276	19,334
Frank Nobilo, New Zealand	69	67	72	68	276	19,334
Ronan Rafferty, N. Ireland	71	66	65	74	276	19,334
Jonathan Lomas, England	66	70	72	68	276	19,334
Russell Claydon, England	72	71	68	65	276	19,334
Larry Mize, USA	73	69	64	70	276	19,334
Greg Norman, Australia	71	67	69	69	276	19,334
Mark Calcavecchia, USA	71	70	67	68	276	19,334
Mark McNulty, Zimbabwe	71	70	68	67	276	19,334
Peter Senior, Australia	68	71	67	71	277	12,500
Mark Brooks, USA	74	64	71	68	277	12,500
Vijay Singh, Fiji	70	68	69	70	277	12,500
Greg Turner, New Zealand	65	71	70	71	277	12,500
Loren Roberts, USA	68	69	69	72	278	7,973
Tom Lehman, USA	70	69	70	69	278	7,973
Peter Jacobsen, USA	69	70	67	72	278	7,973
Andrew Coltart, Scotland	71	69	66	72	278	7,973
Paul Lawrie, Scotland	71	69	70	68	278	7,973
Bob Estes, USA	72	68	72	66	278	7,973
Mike Springer, USA	72	67	68	71	278	7,973
Craig Stadler, USA	71	69	66	72	278	7,973
Ernie Els, South Africa	69	69	69	71	278	7,973
Jeff Maggert, USA	69	74	67	68	278	7,973
Terry Price, Australia	74	65	71	68	278	7,973
Lee Janzen, USA	74	69	69	67	279	6,700
Gary Evans, England	69	69	73	68	279	6,700
Mark Davis, England	75	68	69	67	279	6,700
Jose Maria Olazabal, Spain	72	71	69	68	280	6,100
Jean Van de Velde, France	68	70	71	71	280	6,100
Darren Clarke, N. Ireland	73	68	69	70	280	6,100
Masashi Ozaki, Japan	69	71	66	74	280	6,100
David Gilford, England	72	68	72	68	280	6,100
Davis Love III, USA	71	67	68	74	280	6,100
Seve Ballesteros, Spain	70	70	71	69	280	6,100
Domingo Hospital, Spain	72	69	71	68	280	6,100
Brian Marchbank, Scotland	71	70	70	69	280	6,100
Howard Twitty, USA	71	72	66	72	281	5,450
David Edwards, USA	68	68	73	72	281	5,450
Jim Gallagher, Jr., USA	73	68	69	71	281	5,450
Greg Kraft, USA	69	74	66	72	281	5,450

Name	R1	R2	R3	R4	Total	Prize
David Frost, South Africa	70	71	71	70	282	4,925
Tsukasa Watanabe, Japan	72	71	68	71	282	4,925
Mats Lanner, Sweden	69	74	69	70	282	4,925
Katsuyoshi Tomori, Japan	69	69	73	71	282	4,925
Tommy Nakajima, Japan	73	68	69	73	283	4,700
John Cook, USA	73	67	70	73	283	4,700
Peter Baker, England	71	72	70	70	283	4,700
Brian Watts, USA	68	70	71	74	283	4,700
Ross McFarlane, England	68	74	67	74	283	4,700
Robert Allenby, Australia	72	69	68	75	284	4,350
Gordon Brand, Jr., Scotland	72	71	73	68	284	4,350
Bernhard Langer, Germany	72	70	70	72	284	4,350
Per-Ulrik Johansson, Sweden	73	69	69	73	284	4,350
Hajime Meshiai, Japan	72	71	71	70	284	4,350
Wayne Grady, Australia	68	74	67	75	284	4,350
Christy O'Connor, Jr., Ireland	71	69	71	73	284	4,350
Lennie Clements, USA	72	71	72	70	285	4,050
Carl Mason, England	69	71	73	72	285	4,050
Steve Elkington, Australia	71	72	73	69	285	4,050
Mark Roe, England	74	68	73	70	285	4,050
Ruben Alvarez, Argentina	70	72	71	72	285	4,050
Wayne Riley, Australia	77	66	70	73	286	3,900
* Warren Bennett, England	72	67	74	73	286	Medal
Sandy Lyle, Scotland	71	72	72	72	287	3,850
Colin Gillies, Scotland	71	70	72	75	288	3,775
Craig Ronald, Scotland	71	72	72	73	288	3,775
Joakim Haeggman, Sweden	71	72	69	77	289	3,650
Ben Crenshaw, USA	70	73	73	73	289	3,650
Craig Parry, Australia	72	68	73	76	289	3,650
Nic Henning, South Africa	70	73	70	78	291	3,550
John Daly, USA	68	72	72	80	292	3,500

NON QUALIFIERS AFTER 36 HOLES
(All professionals receive £600)

Name	R1	R2	Total
Kevin Stables, Scotland	74	70	144
Howard Clark, England	71	73	144
John Huston, USA	71	73	144
Paul McGinley, Ireland	71	73	144
Chris Gray, Australia	69	75	144
Miguel Martin, Spain	69	75	144
Paul Way, England	73	71	144
Mikael Krantz, Sweden	70	74	144
Costantino Rocca, Italy	73	71	144
D.A. Weibring, USA	72	72	144
Jose Rivero, Spain	72	72	144
Stephen Robertson, England	75	70	145
Barry Lane, England	73	72	145
Jack Nicklaus, USA	72	73	145
Tony Johnstone, Zimbabwe	75	70	145
Michael Campbell, N. Zealand	72	73	145
* Lee James, England	75	70	145
Eduardo Romero, Argentina	73	72	145
Miguel Angel Jimenez, Spain	71	74	145
Gary Player, South Africa	72	73	145
Andre Bossert, South Africa	74	72	146
Bradley Hughes, Australia	72	74	146
Scott Simpson, USA	73	73	146
Michael Clayton, Australia	71	75	146
Steven Richardson, England	69	77	146
Peter Mitchell, England	74	72	146
Fulton Allem, South Africa	73	73	146
Mike Harwood, Australia	77	69	146
Wayne Westner, South Africa	73	74	147
Gabriel Hjertstedt, Sweden	71	76	147
Craig Jones, Australia	71	76	147
Bruce Vaughan, USA	69	78	147
Paul Curry, England	73	74	147
Andrew Magee, USA	67	80	147
Lee Trevino, USA	75	72	147
Sam Torrance, Scotland	74	73	147
Kirk Triplett, USA	71	76	147
Hiroshi Goda, Japan	71	76	147
Paul Broadhurst, England	73	75	148
Jim McGovern, USA	78	70	148
Gary Orr, Scotland	76	72	148
Francis Quinn, USA	77	71	148
Gary Emerson, England	75	73	148
Payne Stewart, USA	74	74	148
Kenneth Walker, Scotland	72	76	148
James Wright, England	71	77	148
Steen Tinning, Denmark	75	73	148
Carlos Franco, Paraguay	72	76	148
Andrew Oldcorn, England	77	71	148
Jose Maria Canizares, Spain	80	69	149
* Craig Evans, Wales	74	75	149
Peter Smith, Australia	73	76	149
Gil Morgan, USA	73	76	149
* John Harris, USA	73	76	149
Des Smyth, Ireland	80	69	149
Fredrik Lindgren, Sweden	78	72	150
Keith Waters, England	75	75	150
Ian Baker-Finch, Australia	73	77	150
Chip Beck, USA	76	75	151
Corey Pavin, USA	75	76	151
Carl Green, England	75	76	151
Pierre Fulke, Sweden	77	75	152
Ian Woosnam, Wales	79	73	152
Phil Mickelson, USA	78	74	152
Craig Cassells, England	77	75	152
Mark Mouland, Wales	76	76	152
Bob Charles, New Zealand	74	79	153
Rodger Davis, Australia	77	76	153
Anders Gillner, Sweden	74	79	153
Paul Eales, England	76	78	154
Joe Higgins, Canada	78	76	154
* Stephen Pullan, England	81	74	155
Eduardo Herrera, Colombia	77	79	156
Andrew George, England	74	83	157
Lee Fickling, England	80	80	160

At Turnberry, one is reminded of Robert Louis Stevenson's opinion of the Monterey Peninsula in California:

'The greatest meeting place of land and water in the world.'

ROUND TURNBERRY AILSA

No. 1 350 Yards, Par 4

This is not perhaps as rigourous a start to a championship course as, say, Muirfield or Royal Birkdale. But the two bunkers restored to the left side of the fairway to balance one opposite number and the reinforced defence of the green by two new bunkers means, even in calm or wind-assisted conditions, a re-thinking of the simple iron-and-wedge strategy.

No. 2 428 Yards, Par 4

The second hole turns back on the opening hole along a ridge and has been strengthened by the introduction of two fairway bunkers to challenge the drive, that on the left slightly in advance of its right-hand partner. The second shot is made deceptive by the amount of dead ground ahead. The professional, with his yardage chart, will be less baffled.

No. 3 462 Yards, Par 4

The course again turns back for the longest of the Ailsa's two-shotters. The drive down a valley is unthreatened by a bunker (the rough should be a more than adequate substitute) and will favour the left side of the fairway. This is because the green is more heavily protected on the right side by two bunkers, than by the solitary sentry to the left.

No. 4 167 Yards, Par 3

This is the start of Turnberry's 'signature' sequence of seven holes which hug the shoreline to the 10th green. Miss the elevated green and it's usually a case of 'over and out' — to the right a bunker and a bank, to the left a steep fall from which the sea, which used to lap its base, has long since retreated.

No. 5 441 Yards, Par 4

The fifth hole was lengthened by some 30 yards for the last Open and converted from a par 5 to a long 4 for the purposes of the Championship. The drive should ideally hold to the right, away from two fairway bunkers and to open up the green, sloping sharply from rear to front.

No. 6 222 Yards, Par 3

The Ailsa's second short hole is much more about power than its first. To be short is to be sold short, and as much club as a driver may be needed to carry the valley, avoid the cavernous bunker on the right, and thread the needle to a precipitous target hedged by three bunkers on its left.

No. 7 528 Yards, Par 5

The first of two long holes starts from an elevated tee to a fairway inclining to the left between rough dunes and up a gradual slope to the green. The conditions prevailing at the time will dictate how much of the dogleg can be bitten off.

No. 8 430 Yards, Par 4

The drive must avoid the bunker to the right of a leftward slanting fairway and also the rough country on the left. The second shot is the more testing, particularly since the well-protected and elevated green is on two levels. A hooked approach could finish on the beach.

No. 9 452 Yards, Par 4

The ninth hole is one of British golf's most photogenic holes. The famous back tee, calling for a drive over a rocky, sea-dashed inlet, was not in the original design. The saddle-back fairway is not easy to hold, but this year the rough on the left side has been trimmed back in the interest of fairness.

No. 10 452 Yards, Par 4

Depending on the direction and strength of the wind, it can take as much as two woods, or a drive and a short iron, to reach the green. The right side of the fairway is the preferable one, but the large central bunker short of the green is more likely to be seen as cosmetic than as a genuine threat.

No. 11 177 Yards, Par 3

The 11th hole has another tee positioned close to the seashore. Although the least exacting of the short holes, tee shots here have been known to clear the left-hand fence out of bounds, the side also favoured for pin positions directly behind a bunker. Prudence may suggest playing for the gap.

No. 12 448 Yards, Par 4

The new tee introduced in time for the 1986 Open stretched the hole by 50 yards. This allowed the bunkers down the left side of the fairway to be brought more into play and added difficulty to the second shot to a contoured green set beneath the war memorial.

No. 13 411 Yards, Par 4

Unless the player is long enough to carry the bunker and grassy hollow in the corner of the right-turning dogleg, the gap to the left offers the safest access to the green. The green is raised and has no guarding bunkers, and the lack of definition in the target creates problems for the approach shot.

No. 14 440 Yards, Par 4

The 14th hole faces into the prevailing wind and is probably the hardest of the two-shot holes. To avoid the solitary bunker on the left, the drive should favour the right half of the fairway, the preferred side since from there the tightly-bunkered green is made more accessible to the second shot.

No. 15 209 Yards, Par 3

This is by no means an easy target, since the lie of the land on the right falls sharply down a bank from the green, which is heavily protected on the left by bunkers. In 1977 Tom Watson holed from off the green for a 2 to draw level with Jack Nicklaus.

No. 16 410 Yards, Par 4

The lone fairway bunker on the left will influence favouring the right side from the tee. Wilson's Burn, not in itself a particularly daunting hazard, still demands avoidance of underclubbing to a green behind which banks and rough territory are as likely to penalize the overstrong.

No. 17 498 Yards, Par 5

The driving area has been tightened since the 1986 Open by the logical step of moving the bunker from the right-hand rough into the fairway. The hole then climbs from a shallow valley through a narrow waist to the green beyond. This was ranked as the least difficult hole in the two previous Championships.

No. 18 432 Yards, Par 4

From the 18th tee of the Arran course the hole becomes a sharp dogleg left, in which corner bunkers and out of bounds persuade players into driving in the opposite direction, towards the embrace of gorse bushes. There are no bunkers round the green, just humps and hollows. In 1986, Greg Norman had one putt for 61, and took three.

TURNBERRY: AGAINST THE ODDS

BY RAYMOND JACOBS

By almost every reasonable measure of sense and sensibility, Turnberry should not exist. Its foundation was questioned, its existence threatened, and its survival challenged. It seems to have undergone more begettings than an Old Testament dynasty. A handful of proprietors have established, nurtured, and expanded the property, which has come through the exigencies imposed upon it by the two World Wars. Their acts of faith in transforming against daunting odds what is, after all, a rather remote dot on the map of Scotland into a resort of international reputation have, in sports terms, seldom been equalled since the difficulties experienced by Job.

This turbulent, unpredictable, and uncertain past has all but been obscured by the way in which the two previous Open Championships were decided. It was almost as if Turnberry's troubled history — despite, as the old Scottish saying has it, everything in its favour being against it — was a justification for the victories, in 1977 and 1986, of Tom Watson and Greg Norman. The heroics they performed were in keeping with the legend of Robert the Bruce, the 14th Century Scottish king whose army almost mythically beat England's at Bannockburn in 1314 after he had taken heart from watching the efforts of a spider to spin a web within the castle whose ruins overlook the ninth fairway.

The dynamics of Watson's defeat of Nicklaus, whom he had already upstaged in the Masters Tournament three months before, were that before he

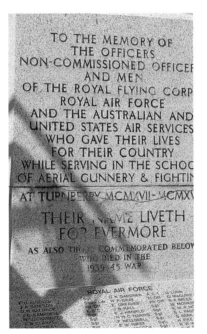

Turnberry has a varied past.

could exult over his one-stroke victory, during the final 36 holes Watson had once been three strokes behind Nicklaus, four times two behind, and four times one behind. The 64 players who completed four rounds had among them 39 scores below 70, yet although the rough was sparse and the weather at its glorious best, two scores of 75 proved good enough to make the 36-hole cut. When, nine years later, the rough was heavier and the weather rougher, the scoring took a similarly mercurial path.

Norman, in that remarkable summer, led all four major championships after three rounds. The Masters, US Open and USPGA Championship proved to be beyond Norman's grasp, but the Open Championship became his first major title. The Australian won by five strokes, his scores of 63 and 69 in the second and fourth rounds contrasting markedly with the 74s he had in the other two rounds. Less than three putts on the home green on Friday would have conferred on Norman the record score for the Open. That that further accolade was not to be was proof of Turnberry's lasting ability to reward great shot-making, but also to withhold favours in any way taken for granted.

Turnberry's own moment of greatest crisis arrived in 1942, when a Torpedo Training Unit was formed there. Three aircraft runways were constructed, having foundations four feet deep covered by six inches of concrete. Ancillary buildings went up, and no one could have seriously believed that golf would ever return to the land which, on the first of Turnberry's

Greg Norman won the 1986 Open by five strokes.

three distinct existences, in 1901, was described as 'likely at last to be turned to the purpose for which it was intended by nature.'

Three men became responsible not only for restoring the two courses, but also for improving their quality. Frank Hole was managing director of British Transport, the post-War owners; Jimmy Alexander, the superintendent of grounds and golf courses; and Philip Mackenzie Ross, the architect. As early as February, 1945, they began their assessment of the requirements. Hangers, stores and administrative offices would have to be demolished. Concrete installations needed to be broken up and excavated. Those that were left, however, became blessings in disguise, as solid foundations for the extensive tentage and car parking, which form an essential part of a modern Open Championship's essential infrastructure.

This formidable trio had first to convince a sceptical government of the day that, even in the straitened circumstances which applied in post-War Britain, the finances should be provided for the work of design and restoration. Indeed, they took only one week to plan the holes and calculate the requirements for grass seed, topsoil and turf. Ross also sketched his initial layout and calculated its probable cost. It was not, however, until August, 1949, that the work began. Less than two years later, the Ailsa course was ready for play, its fairways having been returfed from the land now occupied by the Arran course, instead of reseeded.

The establishing of Turnberry — which preceded, as if in some morality tale, its development, destruction and resurrection — had begun much earlier. Willie Fernie, the professional-greenkeeper at Troon (whose son, Tom, was Turnberry's first professional) was responsible for laying out the courses on land which was the property of the Marquis of Ailsa's Culzean (pronounced Cull-ain) Estate. A few years later the Glasgow and South Western Railway Company built the hotel on the bluff above the courses. The views of the building, with its distinctive terracotta coloured roof above white walls, and from it across the Firth of Clyde towards Arran, Ailsa Craig and the Mull of Kintyre, are among the most appealing in all of golf.

The remains of aircraft runways are still visible on the Turnberry links.

Even before the First World War, Turnberry's qualities had been recognized by holding the first of three Scottish professional championships there, in 1911, and the first of three British women's championships, the following year. But in 1916, not for the last time, war overtook Turnberry. The club's minute book of December, 1916, recorded in the matter-of-fact manner of the time: 'The War Department proposed to take over the golf courses and the clubhouse almost immediately and in these circumstances the committee recommended that the members remove their clubs and personal belongings as early as possible.' Less than three years later, as non-committally, it was noted: 'As the club mistress has now been demobilized, the clubhouse will be reopened on Saturday.'

On runways surfaced with coarse grass, instructional courses were conducted for fighter reconnaissance pilots and their gunners, daylight bomber crews and single-seat fighter pilots. Despite this short-term existence as a training base, there was considerable loss of life. The memorial above the 12th green commemorates the deaths of 35 men from Britain and the Commonwealth and four from the United States. Live ammunition was fired at towed targets, dog-fights were simulated with instructors as the enemy,

and the more reckless among the pilots relieved any tendencies towards boredom by flying upside down past the front of the hotel below the level of the roofline.

That diversionary practice ended with a fatal accident, the ironic fate as it happened, of the outstanding flyer to be stationed at Turnberry, James McCudden, VC, who had survived 870 hours of combat when a pilot's life expectancy averaged no more than 200 hours. He had shot down 57 enemy aircraft. He was killed in France in 1918, not by enemy action but by crashing into woods while attempting a roll at insufficient altitude. Two of McCudden's brothers were also killed flying, and their mother subsequently represented bereaved British women at the ceremonial burial of America's Unknown Soldier at Arlington Cemetery.

Between the wars Turnberry continued to be chosen for championships, notably by the ladies who preceded the gentlemen by many years in selecting Ayrshire links. Two British and five Scottish women's titles were decided. Joyce Wethered in 1921 lost to Cecil Leitch — her only defeat in the total of 10 British and English finals she reached — and Jessie Anderson (later Valentine) in 1939 won the second of her six Scottish championships.

The lighthouse sits above the castle ruins.

During these inter-war years the Ailsa and Arran courses had become the property of London Midland and Scottish Railways, and the company decided they needed to be modernized. Major C.K. Hutchison was called in. He had been runner-up in the Amateur Championship of 1909 and subsequently assisted James Braid, winner of the Open Championship five times in 10 years from 1901, in the creation of the courses at Gleneagles Hotel and in the reconstruction of the Carnoustie championship course.

Hutchison reduced the number of blind shots and increased Ailsa's length, but the work had hardly been completed, in 1938, when the Second World War broke out. Henry Longhurst's nostalgia for the place — that 'with nothing to do but "sit and think" I often used to find myself sitting and thinking of the time when we might once again be playing golf at Turnberry' — seemed unlikely to be requited.

The decision to re-enlist the links to the war effort looks in hindsight to have been particularly perverse, for the area was regarded by pilots in the Royal Air Force as being too dangerous for flight operations. But desk-bound opinion thought otherwise, and prevailed. Accidents regularly happened, because of the cramped nature of the terrain, the incidence of air pockets, flyers who lacked experience, and inadequate standards of aircraft maintenance. On one fine summer's night, apparently no fewer than five aircraft fell into the Firth of Clyde because their pilots could not distinguish between the shore and the sea.

Understandably, post-War competition resumed slowly. For example, John Panton, the Ryder Cup player, in 1954 and 1959, won two of his eight Scottish professional championships, but the event which began seriously to direct the Ailsa toward its present eminence and drew the interest of a wider golfing audience was an event now sadly defunct, the British professional match-play championship. Start-

The five-star Turnberry Hotel offers a magnificent view of the golf courses.

The 441-yard fifth is the second of seven holes that hug the shoreline to the 10th green.

ing in 1957 the tournament was held there at three-yearly intervals and, by coincidence, the respective winners were all players who nearly won the Open — Christy O'Connor, Eric Brown and Dave Thomas. On the heels of that level of recognition, other events formed an orderly queue to enjoy perhaps Britain's most spectacular course.

That setting, with Ailsa Craig, Arran and the Mull of Kintyre forming an unusual sea-bound backdrop, attracted the men's Home Internationals in 1960 and the next year Michael Bonallack, the present Secretary of the Royal and Ancient Golf Club, won the first of his five Amateur Championships. In 1963 Britain and Ireland looked as if they would win the Walker Cup for only the second time when they led by three points after the first day's play. However, the United States postponed those celebrations for another eight years with an irresistible counter-attack, but the Ailsa's reputation as a magnificent challenge was by now thoroughly established and sponsors of professional tournaments responded.

Their shelf-life would be short, however. For instance, Braemar's seven-club tournament, won by Ryder Cup player Lionel Platts, was held only once, in 1964. Another tournament, also abandoned subsequently, the John Player Classic, was won by Bob Charles, the New Zealand left-hander, and Charles Coody, the 1971 US Masters champion. In 1979 Sandy Lyle won the European Open.

At Turnberry, one is reminded of Robert Louis Stevenson's opinion of the Monterey Peninsula, on whose shores lie the Pebble Beach and Cypress Point courses. 'The greatest meeting place of land and water in the world,' the Scottish writer described the merging of cliffs, rocks, sand and ocean. If the Ailsa course cannot quite measure up to northern California's spectacular confluence, it has surely developed a character unique to these islands — the consequence of faith, hope and perspicacity and sustained by its latest proprietors, the Japanese company, Nitto Kogyo, in their £10 million investment to expand the resort's facilities and construct a new clubhouse. The founders' spirit lives on.

A new clubhouse was built before the 1994 Open.

Harry Vardon emphasized the importance of body movement and footwork in the golf swing.

HARRY VARDON:
THE COMPLETE GOLFER

BY MICHAEL McDONNELL

For a moment, at least, a remote figure wandered back through the mists of time and hung around Turnberry as if to claim a perpetual relevance and underline the truth that there is an unbroken link between the deeds of our modern heroes and those of the historical characters who preceded them.

Indeed the quality and worth of any achievement can only be judged by what has been accomplished previously, so that progress in sport has to be accessed in terms of precedent and none more so than in golf itself. Accordingly, when Tom Watson edged his way back from the margins of the record books to present the prospect of perhaps a sixth Open title, he stirred thoughts of Harry Vardon and the homage still due to the only golfer in history ever to attain the magical half dozen.

But in a sense winning on such a grand scale was but the secondary achievement to emerge from the life and times of the Complete Golfer. In fact the irony is that this accumulation of glittering prizes serves more as evidence of a greater contribution he made to the game. It was another part of an equation that made him arguably the most important figure in the history of the game.

Harry Vardon gave the game the modern golf swing. His personal style and technique established a form and orthodoxy by which it has been played ever since, all over the world and by the greatest performers of every era. Yet the extraordinary truth is there had been no great mission behind this discovery. No tantalising dream of perfection nor thoughts of a better way propelled this former gardener from the island of Jersey in the English Channel into the most pivotal prominence in the development of golf.

He took the golf swing from its lunging boisterous seashore origins and gave it a precision and method that worked effectively no matter how the terrain over which it was played might vary. He brought standard and pattern to playing the game, and in so doing evolved a method which in the hundred years and more since he first held a club in his massive hands has not been fundamentally changed despite developments in human physique and golf equipment.

It was all unwitting, of course. When the boy gardener accompanied his employer Major Spofforth over the links in Jersey in 1880, there was no greater personal ambition than eventually to become Head Gardener, marry a local and settle down.

And yet in some idle moment while waiting upon the Major, he had swung at the gutta percha golf ball with a style that differed from all the rest. For some reason of physique, he eschewed the old flaying style that was standard practice within the game. Instead, he stood close to the ball with a narrow stance and seemed to pick the club up in the backswing in what was a slow and methodical style that even allowed him to bend his left arm at the top.

The result was amazing because the ball was lofted into the air without any loss of power. In effect, Vardon had brought about a complete transformation in the striking of a golf ball, and in so doing dictated forever the manner in which the sport would be played. Quite simply, he had discovered a way to play the all-air golf stroke which was not therefore subject to the vagaries of bounce or bunkers that beset the traditional seaside swipe, but instead could soar majestically over every peril to find the safety and sanctuary of the green. Moreover, he had adapted a style of overlapping grip that was already being employed in those days by J.H. Taylor and Leslie Balfour Melville, but which would become linked with Vardon's name because of the success he achieved.

Therein lies another truth; the effectiveness of any method can only be measured by the success it

Vardon tees off as Old Tom Morris (far left) observes.

achieves, and in Vardon's case it depended on the number and quality of his victories so that cause and effect became interlinked. And yet it was a style that endured so effectively that at the age of 50, in the sweltering heat of Inverness, he came agonizingly close to winning the 1920 US Open for the second time in a championship career that had already spanned 18 years. On that occasion it was his stamina rather than technique that gave out, because throughout his life Vardon suffered from bouts of tuberculosis and was at one time forced to undergo months of treatment in a sanatorium. For all that, he refused to relinquish his pipe-smoking and could even swing effectively with the pipe in his mouth.

He was without question the superstar of his day. His money matches against fellow professionals attracted thousands of spectators. His tours of the United States giving exhibitions and playing money matches were always massive sell-outs. In one Chicago department store, the entire stock of golf equipment was sold out in a day after Vardon hit a few golf balls into a practice net.

Such was the widespread appeal of the man that he was offered lucrative contracts to leave Britain and live in the United States, where he could have become a millionaire and where his fragile health might

have become more robust. But he declined and went home to his family and friends and the life he knew in Britain.

He was both vulnerable and sensitive, and these traits at times served to affect the manner in which he played. During one money match at St Andrews, in which he partnered J.H. Taylor against Sandy Herd and James Braid, he became so upset at the partisan behaviour of the local crowd that he wanted to quit until Taylor insisted they play on, and eventually they beat their rivals 12 up in the subsequent match at Troon.

But on another occasion, when Vardon was taken seriously ill with a recurrence of tuberculosis on the eve of a match, he refused to quit and instead partnered Taylor to a massive victory. In fact these two campaigners who, along with James Braid, made up the Great Triumvirate which dominated the game up until the First World War, first met in a challenge match which Vardon won.

Then Vardon went on to foil Taylor's chance of an Open hat-trick by winning a play-off at Muirfield in 1896 to start a string of championship wins that would endure until 1914. During that time, too, he won the US Open in 1900 and lost the 1913 US Open in a play-off along with Ted Ray to an 18-

year-old Boston sports store clerk named Francis Ouimet, who became the first native-born American to capture the title.

By the time the First World War had ended, the British domination had waned and given way to an American strength that was to endure at championship level for decades to come, even though the standards and style set by Vardon continued to influence the game.

His method of striking was so repetitive it gave rise to Hogan-like fables about his ability; for example, that he disliked playing 36 holes a day because it inevitably meant he landed in divot holes he had created in the morning. But it is a fact that he could hit three woods repeatedly within four feet of the hole and nominate beforehand which side of the flagstick the golf balls would land. He was, in the opinion of his old foe and close friend J.H. Taylor, 'the finest and most finished golfer the game has produced.'

Vardon's own philosophy was as simplistic but effective, and he insisted, 'It is cause and effect. It is all in the hands of the player to make of it what he will. Every good shot and the bad are of your own making.' There was, therefore, never an excuse for losing. No complaining nor grumbling about bad luck. All he would say after any defeat was simply, 'I played my game, Sir. I played my game.' It was, after all, the best he could do on the day.

His ideas on golf technique might at first seem trapped in their own times because he argued that a man played his best golf wearing a buttoned-up jacket, and that braces to hold up trousers were also beneficial to the golf swing. What, in effect, he was emphasising was the importance of body movement and footwork in the golf swing, which is as fundamental to success now as it was then.

Perhaps the other testimony to Vardon's technique was that it coped effectively and without diminution during the period when golf itself underwent the massive change-over from solid gutty ball to the rubber-cored wound Haskell ball, which produced a different flight and achieved greater distance. Vardon won championships with both kinds of golf ball, although he had completed his reign using only

The Great Triumvirate: J.H. Taylor, James Braid and Vardon won the Open Championship 16 times in 21 years.

hickory clubs before the steel shafts were sanctioned in 1929.

In any case, Vardon's contribution to the game stretched far beyond an accumulation of titles that might serve to test the prowess and ambition of every performer who followed and give a sobering perspective to real achievement. The record book, after all, remains the only inflexible standard by which golfers of each generation can be judged.

The greatest legacy that a man can leave is that his field of endeavour is somehow better because he was involved; that it has advanced and improved simply because of his touch. It is a safe judgement that can be applied to Vardon. In modern times only Peter Thomson and Tom Watson have come close to equalling his collection of Open titles with five each.

No matter. The Vardon legacy provides a reason to keep trying. And that too is a tribute to the Complete Golfer. Not only did he set the target for others to follow. He provided the means for them to do it, too. And above all, he played his game, Sir. He played his game. So, too, do we, Sir. So too do we.

Jonathan Lomas (66) said, 'To do well in the Open was a dream.'

DAY

1

LOW SCORES ARE THE RULE

BY ROBERT SOMMERS

Because it was such a defining moment in the game's chronicles, memories of the 1977 Open Championship command our thoughts whenever we return to Turnberry, reminding us that on those four glorious days Tom Watson and Jack Nicklaus raised golf to heights we could only have dreamed of a few days earlier.

Reflections on those times evidently command Watson's thoughts as well. Before the 1994 championship began, he called Nicklaus and told him he had arranged a match for their final practice round. It was against Greg Norman, the defending Open champion, and Nick Price, who many believe had been playing better golf than anyone over the year since Norman blistered Royal St George's with 64 in the last round of the 1993 Open.

That Watson and Nicklaus shot a better-ball score of about 60 and whipped the younger men stirred some hopes that this might indeed turn out to be 1977 all over again. It wasn't; nor could it be. Sensing the illusion their great round had created, Nicklaus said, 'A lot of people think you're going to be around forever. That can't happen. A lot of people out there today thought it was 1977. It isn't.'

Nicklaus was right about himself, but only partly right about Watson. Jack fought his way round Turnberry in 72, two over par, but Watson, reliving his past glories, shot 68, not good enough to lead but good enough to rank him among the leaders.

The day ended with three unlikely players at the top. Greg Turner, a 31-year-old New Zealander, led

Greg Turner's 65 included two eagles.

with 65. He was followed by Jonathan Lomas, a young professional from Shropshire just beginning to make his way on the PGA European Tour, and by Andrew Magee, from the United States. Lomas shot 66 and Magee 67.

This was a day of unusually low scoring. In addition to those three, 11 men shot 68 and 16 others shot 69. Watson was, of course, among the 68 shooters, along with Jesper Parnevik, who was to play an increasingly important role as the championship progressed; David Feherty, who would as well, and John Daly, who wouldn't. Peter Senior, who tied for fourth place last year, also shot 68. Those at 69 included Price, Ernie Els and Brad Faxon.

Norman, not only the defending champion but the winner in 1986, when the championship visited Turnberry for the second time, shot 71, along with Mark Calcavecchia, who had beaten him in a play-off for the 1989 championship at Royal Troon and remains the only American champion since Watson's last victory, in 1983 at Royal Birkdale. Three times the champion, Seve Ballesteros, shot level-par 70.

Finding 30 men under par shouldn't have been surprising in this age when scores that might have seemed remarkable a few years ago have become commonplace. Furthermore, Turnberry was ripe for scoring. Weekend rains had softened its greens, the fairways had been widened somewhat from 1986, when the widest measured little more than 22 yards, and everyone agreed the course itself had never been better conditioned.

Jean Van de Velde (68) had four bogeys.

Andrew Magee (67) made putts of 20 and 35 feet.

Gary Emerson hit the first shot of the 123rd Open Championship.

Loren Roberts (68) was four under par after 14 holes.

Peter Senior (68) birdied three of the last six holes.

What was needed, moaned those who feel more comfortable when the game's best players must struggle for their scores, was a touch of weather. Wednesday had been a calm, warm and sunny day, a day to cherish on Scottish coastal land, but a brisk wind began to rise just as the first group left the tee for the first round. Those who went out early had the best the day would offer, for conditions worsened in the afternoon, until finally those who went out after noon played through miserable weather. Rain fell steadily, and the temperature plunged.

As a consequence, players found themselves using clubs they wouldn't ordinarily have played. For example, Bernhard Langer and Payne Stewart teed off at 10.15. With the rising wind coming out of the south, they played the third hole directly into the breeze. Ordinarily players of this calibre reach the greens of 460-yard holes with clubs to spare; even a 550-yard hole is reachable with their second shots under calm conditions. Here, though, they both played wooden clubs. Neither man reached the green. Others had similar experiences on the 17th, which nearly everyone reached with irons for their second shots in the later stages. Loren Roberts, Costantino Rocca and Lee James, the Amateur champion, all used woods for their second shots and all fell short.

Standing on the tee of the second hole, which played downwind, Turner pulled out his three wood and asked his caddie if he thought he could reach a set of bunkers about 280 yards out. The caddie said, 'No.' Turner hit his drive beyond them.

Watson had been playing a nine iron to the 16th in his practice rounds, and yet he needed a five iron in the first round.

Without question those who played early had the advantage, before the rain began falling in the early afternoon. Predictably, some players suggested the field should be split, half starting from the first tee and half from the 10th. If they believed the Royal and Ancient Golf Club of St Andrews would take it seriously, Michael Bonallack, the club's Secretary, ended speculation by reminding everyone that this is a championship, not just a tournament.

In a championship it is essential that everyone play the holes in the same sequence, that everyone begin Turnberry in the same manner, play the first hole into the wind, then the second downwind, back into the wind for the third, then the long downwind slog from the fourth through the eighth, building up to the final crescendo of the 15th, 16th, 17th and 18th all in their proper order.

The players complain that not everyone plays the

Ernie Els said, '69 was the best I could have scored.'

Ross McFarlane (68) was a surprise among the leaders.

same course under the same conditions. Starting on both the first and 10th wouldn't accomplish that goal anyway. If the weather were to change as it changed during the first round at Turnberry, half the field would play under different conditions no matter how the field might be divided.

Nevertheless, it is true that those in the afternoon played under more difficult conditions, but at the same time it is equally true that Turner was among those late starters. He began at 2.15, just behind Norman, Calcavecchia and Ian Woosnam, and just as the rain began falling more heavily.

Turner had first come to international attention by playing for New Zealand in the 1984 World Amateur Team Championship in Hong Kong. He turned to professional golf soon after he returned home and joined the PGA European Tour two years later. He won his first tournament in his first year, but waited seven years to win his second, the 1993 Lancia Martini Italian Open.

Turner had shown signs of awakening in the weeks leading up to the Open. With a lower score in each round, he played the Murphy's Irish Open in 73, 70, 69 and 66, and tied for fourth place with 278, then shot 65 and 67 in the Open's qualifying rounds.

Even though Turner played Turnberry in five un-

John Daly (68) thought the wind was to his advantage.

der par, his round could be called slightly bizarre. It was made up of two eagles, three birdies, two bogeys and 11 pars. Turner began calmly enough with five consecutive pars, missing only the third green, where he holed from 15 feet to save par. Playing the 222-yard sixth downwind, Greg needed no more than a five iron. He laid it within 15 feet and holed once more.

Next he came to the seventh, a 528-yard par 5 that played downwind as well. Playing a three wood from the tee, he followed with a four iron that rolled within five feet of the flagstick. Once again a putt fell and Turner had gone three under par.

Two more routine pars and Turner had gone out in 32. Now, though, he faced the long battle home with so many holes playing into the wind and rain. He ran into his first taste of trouble on the 12th, a 448-yard par 4 with a subtly deceptive approach

Brian Watts (68) birdied the 16th and 17th holes.

Frank Nobilo (69) celebrated a holed shot.

Katsuyoshi Tomori (69) matched Masashi Ozaki.

Greg Norman (71) 'did not play very well.'

Nick Faldo (75) played the wrong ball on the 17th hole.

that plays perhaps a club longer than it looks. His one-iron second shot missed the green and he bogeyed from six feet.

Greg won back a stroke on the hard 14th with a seven iron to five feet, but he lost it on the 15th where he bunkered his one-iron tee shot and bogeyed. He was two under then with three holes to go.

Now he played the key hole of the round, the 16th, a par 4 of 410 yards that is usually no more than a drive and a pitch. With the wind coming directly against him, Turner hit a fine drive that pulled up 178 yards from the pin.

Feeling the strength of the wind, he knew he would need a substantial club, perhaps even a two iron, which he normally hits about 220 yards. Checking, Turner asked his caddie if he thought the two iron would be too much club. The caddie said, 'No,' once more, and added, 'It's just right.' The caddie knew what he was talking about here. Turner lashed into the shot and watched it bore through the wind, hit short of the flagstick, run directly toward the hole, then dive in. A second eagle. Now he stood four under par with two holes to play. More was coming.

Two woods left him still short of the 17th green, and his pitch looked a feeble effort in any company. It flopped on the green and ran 20 feet from the cup. Still, sometimes scores are meant to be. He rolled it in for the birdie. Five under now, he played a driver and a two iron on to the 18th green and two-putted from 25 feet. With 33 on the extremely difficult homeward nine, Turner had his 65 and had taken the lead from Lomas.

Just 26 years old, Lomas was playing in his first Open Championship, and while he remained at the top only a short time, he didn't stray very far from the leaders and indeed had a very good finish that justified his long struggle to succeed in professional golf. He tried four times to qualify for the PGA European Tour until finally making it this year, and had finished among the top six in four events, the latest the Bell's Scottish Open the week before the Open Championship, where he tied for fifth place.

Although he stands 5-ft-9, he looks much shorter as he stands up to the ball with his driver in hand. This is an illusion. Where the most common drivers

With Ailsa Craig framing the background, Anders Forsbrand completed his opening-round 72.

measure 43½ inches to 44 inches in length, Lomas's measures 47 inches. It is difficult to use, to be sure, but he claims the longer arc has added about 20 yards to his drives until now he can hit the ball about 280 yards. In this era of power golf, he needs it.

It was not his driving, though, but his work around the greens that led to his low score. Beginning at 9.25 under relatively mild conditions, Lomas missed three of the first four greens and yet gave away nothing. He played delicate chip shots inside three feet on each of them and saved his pars. He made his first birdie on the seventh, which would be vulnerable all day, but Lomas did not reach the green with his six-iron second shot. Rather, he chipped within a foot and of course ran the putt down. He holed his only putt of any length on the ninth, where a 25-footer dropped, and he was out in 33 with five one-putt greens.

Using a putter he had adopted only a week earlier, Lomas one-putted three more coming home, holing from 25 feet once again on the 10th — two 25-footers on consecutive holes — from six inches on the 14th for another birdie, and then saving a par from 10 feet on the 16th.

He escaped with a par 5 on the 17th where he attempted to play a one iron from the matty rough and smothered the shot. A seven iron reached the green and he was down in two for the 5.

An engaging young man with sandy hair and an open face, Lomas floated off the final green on a cloud and said, 'To do well in the Open was a dream.'

Watson shared the same dream with a major codicil; in his mind, to do well would mean to win. Off among the very early starters, at 7.35, he had hardly slept through the night and had been up since 5 o'clock, waiting to begin. He started off quietly enough with two routine pars, then almost pitched in for a birdie after missing the third green. He had his first uncomfortable moment on the sixth, where he left his four iron 60 feet from the hole and three-putted.

One over par now, he made it up with a big drive on the seventh that left him only a six iron into the green. Two putts and he had pulled back to even par.

He still stood even after the 12th, and then ran in a 30-foot putt on the 13th and followed with a pitch to six feet on the 17th. These are the putts that have troubled Watson through his decline from the game's pinnacle. Where once they were hardly worth men-

Leading Americans Payne Stewart (top left) and Lee Janzen (bottom) failed to challenge, but newcomer Greg Kraft shot 69.

tioning, they have bothered him for years. Here he rolled it in, and then had a chance to add still another birdie on the 18th. A four-iron approach shot left him within six feet of the cup, but here he missed.

Still, his 68 left him in prime position for a serious run at the championship.

Where Watson stepped off the golf course holding high hopes, a number of other players of quality had trouble, particularly Nick Faldo. Clearly not the player he had been a year ago when he had played such marvellous golf at Sandwich and yet had been caught and passed by Norman's closing 64, Faldo had played an undistinguished Masters, placing 32nd, and had played so badly at Oakmont he had missed the 36-hole cut in the US Open. Starting just before 2 o'clock, grouped with Els, the young South African who had won the US Open a month earlier, and Jim McGovern, Faldo played a listless sort of round through the first 16 holes, making no birdies and taking two bogeys, both on the first nine.

Two over par then, he pushed his drive into the right rough on the 17th, and so did McGovern. Not the longest hitter in the game, Faldo found a ball short of where McGovern was looking for his and played it. It turned out to have been McGovern's ball. Faldo hadn't checked and admitted he had seen only a white blotch. It seemed totally out of charac

Jose Maria Olazabal (72) had a double bogey.

Scottish favourite Sam Torrance shot 74.

ter for a player so meticulous as Faldo, for only a glimpse would have shown him the ball wasn't his. McGovern was playing a different brand.

McGovern found a ball and saw it belonged to Faldo. The mistake cost Nick a two-stroke penalty under Rule 15-3, and he had to play his own ball (McGovern replaced his ball on the spot where Faldo had played it). With the two-stroke penalty, Faldo made 8 and shot 75, clearly putting himself at risk of missing the cut.

He was not alone. Ian Woosnam, who has fallen from among the ranks of the game's leading players, shot 79 and had little or no hope of playing through 72 holes; and Phil Mickelson, the young American who has shown promise occasionally but has played some awful stuff as well, shot 78.

Jose Maria Olazabal played some dull golf and shot 72, along with Colin Montgomerie, Langer and, of course, Nicklaus. Ian Baker-Finch, the 1991 champion, slipped to 73, along with John Cook, who had nearly won at Muirfield two years earlier. Corey Pavin, the Toyota World Match Play champion who tied for fourth in the 1993 Open, shot 75. Lee Janzen, the 1993 US Open champion, and Payne Stewart, who had won the US Open in 1991 and placed second to Janzen in 1993, both shot 74 and were never heard from again.

Bernhard Langer (72) discusses strategy.

FIRST ROUND RESULTS

HOLE	1	2	3	4	5	6	7	8	9	10	11	12	13	14	15	16	17	18	
PAR	4	4	4	3	4	3	5	4	4	4	3	4	4	4	3	4	5	4	TOTAL
Greg Turner	4	4	4	3	4	2	3	4	4	4	3	5	4	3	4	2	4	4	65
Jonathan Lomas	4	4	4	3	4	3	4	4	3	3	3	4	4	3	3	4	5	4	66
Andrew Magee	4	4	4	3	4	3	4	4	4	4	2	5	3	3	4	5	3	4	67
Tom Watson	4	4	4	3	4	4	4	4	4	4	3	4	3	4	3	4	4	4	68
Loren Roberts	3	4	4	3	4	3	4	4	4	4	3	4	3	3	4	4	6	4	68
Jean Van de Velde	3	5	5	3	4	4	3	4	4	3	2	5	4	4	3	4	5	3	68
Peter Senior	4	4	5	2	4	3	5	4	4	4	3	5	3	4	3	3	4	4	68
David Edwards	4	4	4	3	3	3	4	4	4	4	3	4	4	4	3	4	5	4	68
John Daly	4	4	4	3	3	3	4	4	3	4	3	5	4	4	4	4	4	4	68
Jesper Parnevik	4	4	5	3	3	3	4	4	4	4	2	5	4	4	2	4	5	4	68
Wayne Grady	3	4	4	3	4	3	4	5	4	4	3	4	4	3	3	5	5	3	68
David Feherty	4	5	4	2	4	2	4	4	4	3	3	4	5	4	3	4	4	5	68
Brian Watts	4	4	5	2	3	3	5	4	4	4	3	4	4	4	4	3	4	4	68
Ross McFarlane	4	3	4	3	5	3	4	4	4	4	2	4	4	4	3	4	5	4	68

HOLE SUMMARY

HOLE	PAR	EAGLES	BIRDIES	PARS	BOGEYS	HIGHER	RANK	AVERAGE
1	4	1	7	106	37	5	7	4.24
2	4	0	28	111	16	1	13	3.96
3	4	0	2	81	72	1	2	4.46
4	3	0	34	116	6	0	17	2.82
5	4	0	26	111	18	1	13	3.96
6	3	0	11	107	38	0	9	3.17
7	5	16	82	51	7	0	18	4.31
8	4	0	6	112	32	6	7	4.24
9	4	0	12	103	38	3	10	4.22
OUT	35	17	208	898	264	17		35.38
10	4	0	26	118	12	0	15	3.91
11	3	0	22	115	19	0	12	2.98
12	4	0	1	58	84	13	1	4.71
13	4	0	7	86	56	7	3	4.43
14	4	1	17	113	23	2	11	4.06
15	3	0	13	83	59	1	4	3.31
16	4	1	12	95	36	12	6	4.31
17	5	1	44	94	16	1	16	4.83
18	4	0	7	93	51	5	5	4.36
IN	35	3	149	855	356	41		36.90
TOTAL	70	20	357	1753	620	58		72.28

Players Below Par	30
Players At Par	8
Players Above Par	118

LOW SCORES

Low First Nine	John Daly	32
	Gabriel Hjertstedt	32
	Greg Turner	32
Low Second Nine	Jonathan Lomas	33
	Andrew Magee	33
	Peter Senior	33
	Greg Turner	33
	Jean Van de Velde	33
	Tom Watson	33
Low Round	Greg Turner	65

Information, news and views of the Open Championship take many forms.

Tom Watson found 'a couple of pigeons' before his practice round with Jack Nicklaus.

RECALLING THE 1977 OPEN

BY MICHAEL WILLIAMS

It was shortly after breakfast on the Tuesday morning that the telephone rang in Jack Nicklaus' suite in the Turnberry Hotel. Tom Watson was on the other end of the line. 'Good morning Jack,' he said, 'I thought I'd tell you I've lined up a couple of pigeons for tomorrow.'

'Oh, yes,' replied Nicklaus, 'and who are they?' he asked as he gazed across the sweeping Ayrshire links out towards Ailsa Craig and the smudge of the Isle of Arran, partly obscured by the grey visibility of a morning that hardly suggested the month of July.

'Norman and Price,' answered Watson, as he grinned to himself. 'Some pigeons,' grunted Nicklaus as he considered the prospect of facing the combined forces of, at the time, the first (Norman) and third (Price) players in the Sony Ranking. It was nevertheless all right by him.

It was also all right by him when not much more than 24 hours later they came off the 18th green, their cash-flow suitably enough enhanced for their respective wives, Barbara Nicklaus and Linda Watson, to make their way to the exhibition tent and each buy a cashmere sweater; 'or maybe just a sleeve' cautioned Nicklaus with his awareness of how expensive these things can be.

No matchmaker could have stage-managed it better. It was a natural. Here were the 'old salts,' Nicklaus at 54, Watson at 44, showing that they still occasionally had a trick or two too many up their sleeves for younger upstarts like Norman and Price. Now they were partners just as, 17 years earlier, they had been protagonists in that duel to end all duels for the 1977 Open Championship, the first time it had been held at Turnberry.

It still seems only yesterday as one recalls that titanic struggle, both of them scoring 68 in the first round, both 70 in the second and then, playing together now, both 65 in the third. By then there were eyes for no one else, so far ahead that no one else mattered. Hubert Green, who was third, described himself as having 'won the other tournament.'

The championship however was won by Watson, with another 65 to Nicklaus' 66, hardly an eyelash between them as they swapped birdie for birdie with an excellence of golf that almost defied belief. They were seemingly inseparable, though the advantage was with Nicklaus when he led by a stroke coming to the short 15th, on the green and Watson wide to the left.

But it was Watson who holed for a 2, with his putter from a sandy lie. In match-play terms it was a two-hole swing and when Nicklaus missed a short putt for a birdie at the 17th, it seemed all over. Not a bit of it.

Having almost driven into the whins at the 18th, Nicklaus made the most of a lie that was better than it might have been, found the edge of the green and then holed the putt for a 3. It was one last defiant gesture; but insufficient. Watson had already hit a seven-iron second shot to two feet or less and, in the stillness that followed the pandemonium, sank the putt to win.

All of this was very much in the minds of Watson and Nicklaus as, that Wednesday afternoon, when the sun at last came out to reveal Turnberry in all its glory, they reminisced over who had done what, where and when all those years ago.

'It was a nostalgic day for us,' reflected Watson. 'We had our picture taken at the ninth with the lighthouse in the background. I hope to get it framed to take home with me.'

Both found it refreshing to be in a 'money match' again. 'We used to play them all the time,' said Watson, 'get a fourball and go out there and play. It made the practice rounds interesting and I miss that. Now in a practice round all they want to do is to hit from different places. Playing for a little cash gets your competitive juices going.'

Watson is as readily identified with Turnberry as the lighthouse itself.

Between them Nicklaus and Watson were something like 10 under par, both of them round in the mid-60s. 'Tom is playing awfully well,' praised Nicklaus. 'He would not be my first choice to win this week but he would certainly be in my top three.'

News travels fast on the grapevine of golf. Overnight the odds against Watson winning a sixth title, to equal the record of Harry Vardon, came down from 50-1 to 22-1. There was a lot of sentiment involved, rather as with Lester Piggott when the Derby comes around each year.

In the jokey atmosphere of a pre-championship press conference with its exchanged compliments ('Jack, too, is playing great') Watson was prepared to tempt some fate when he said 'you can put your money on me' but what he was not, at this stage, prepared to do was confide the putting tip he had been given by Lee Trevino when the two of them, and their wives, played a little golf in Ireland en route to Scotland.

'That's my business,' he retorted to his questioner, though by the time another day had passed we knew it was nothing more than pushing his hands a little more forward. Nonetheless it was feeling comfortable for someone who, in his day, had been the most deadly of putters and had even produced a whole book on it.

But putting is not only about the stroke but also what is going on in the mind, the fear of failure being something that, as the years pass, invades the mind and breeds the twitch, or yips as it tends to be termed in America. It had a lot to do with Watson not

having won a tournament since 1987, let alone an Open since 1983.

Yet, through it all, Watson may have changed putters but never his basic method. He knows all about putting cross-handed (left below right), the Bernhard Langer-style as he clamps his left forearm to the shaft with his right hand, and also the broom-handled putter that, like croquet putting, ought to have been banned. If one crosses the boundaries of what constitutes golf so, in my opinion, does the other.

There have been no such resorts by Watson. 'I think I am just too stubborn,' he reflects, bound to the belief that what once worked must surely work again. There was not much on Thursday, the opening day of the championship, to suggest otherwise. Watson began with 68, just as he had those 17 years ago. It was tempting to believe that he was on the march again.

His morning call had come early, at 5 am, which it had to be for a 7.35 starting time, a sign perhaps that the Royal and Ancient, unlike those who had hastily put their money on him, no longer regarded him as a likely contender. Certainly Watson could never remember teeing off as early as that in the Open, but he was excited enough about his golf not to have slept well.

Even with some breakfast inside him and a warm-up on the practice ground, he still felt as if he had some cobwebs in his eyes when he stood on the first tee, and he might have been disconcerted to find the wind blowing from south, which meant that the first and third holes were dead into it.

Consequently, the outward half was the easier of the two. 'That's where I thought the scoring would come from,' said Watson later, 'but I didn't get the job done from there.' He was out in level par with one birdie and one bogey but, coming home with the wind, he raised his game with two birdies and no bogeys.

'A 68 was a fair reflection of the way I played,' said Watson. 'I didn't have too much difficulty with the course, even with the wind. I kept the ball in play, though I did not consistently get it too close to the hole either.'

Nicklaus and Watson recalled old times.

A rather wild one iron from the first tee was not destructive, nor was an errant four-iron second to the third, for he pitched close from 40 yards to save par. His only slip of the day was at the sixth, that long short hole. Watson hit the green with a four iron but right at the back and he three-putted, leaving the first a good 10 feet short.

Watson got the shot back immediately, though it should have been two. He needed only a six-iron second to the par-5 seventh downwind, hit it to five feet and missed the putt. Birdie nonetheless.

Once upon a time Watson would have had no trouble in converting such a chance and one was to be reminded of this susceptibility at this range further on in the round. Not unusually, the longer putts hold no such terrors. He got down in two from a long way at the 12th green, and he bottled one of 30 feet for a 3 at the 13th.

By now the wind was stretching the flags above the grandstands, and Watson found himself needing a two iron to reach the green at the short 15th and a five-iron second to the 16th beyond Wilson's Burn at the foot of the steep slope of the green. In practice it had been a nine iron.

What was so striking about Watson was his relaxed manner, almost as if he was playing a practice round. In his tweed cap, green sweater and brown corduroy slacks, he looked more of the club golfer than an American who has won upwards of $7 million.

His third and last birdie came at the 17th where, after driving into the light rough wide of the new bunker, he hit a four iron short and then, into wind, knocked a low pitch which screwed to a halt flag high, perhaps six feet to the right. Thankfully he got the putt in.

Down the 18th one saw the best and worst of Watson. It was a testing drive but he took the bold line, just clearing the bunkers at the corner of the dogleg, and that left him with a four-iron second, a towering shot which seemed to hang in the sky forever before plummeting vertically six feet from the flag. His two partners, David Frost and Paul Curry, both hit woods for their seconds, which gives some indication of how long the hole was playing.

No two shots deserved a birdie better than that, but Watson, with the chance of 67, hit what he readily admitted to have been 'a lousy stroke' that never looked like going in. 'I just have to accept that sort of thing these days,' he said afterwards philosophically. 'But I am not going to give up, that's for sure.'

He is unshaken in his belief that he can, and will, win again. 'It is just a case of when,' he claims. By the Friday night, it began to look as if it could well be very soon as he repeated the 65 he had had in his last two rounds in 1977. It had the looks of his lucky number as once again he bestrode the Turnberry stage. But there were still two acts of the play to be performed and when finally the curtain fell it was another who took the bow.

The putts were falling for Tom Watson, whose 65 included seven birdies and putts of 20 and 50 feet.

A DAY FILLED WITH CONTRASTS

BY ROBERT SOMMERS

At the close of the first day's play, hardly anyone expected the scoreboard to look quite the same again, as indeed it wouldn't, because so many of those near the top did not have the experience to stay there. At the same time hardly anyone expected the second round to develop as it did either, with the first day's leaders falling from grace — indeed Andrew Magee fell all the way out of the championship — and Tom Watson arousing improbable dreams by roaring to the top of the standing.

It was a day filled with contrasts, a day when Nick Price shot 66 and showed he must still be reckoned with; when Jesper Parnevik birdied three of the last four holes, shot 66 as well, and made a move that would lead to a brush with glory; when Fuzzy Zoeller and Brad Faxon began their climbs, Faxon with a bogey-free 65 and Zoeller with a round of 66 with birdies on each of the par-3 holes; and a day when Nick Faldo showed the

Watson's lead was widely applauded.

value of pride by rearranging his shattered game and climbing back into the championship with 66, another of his stunning bursts of scoring.

On the dimmer side, it was a day as well when John Daly ruined what had been a promising start with two badly played holes and never recovered.

Even the weather was different. Rain had given way to bright, clear skies on the morning of the second round. Every crevice showed on Ailsa Craig, the giant chunk of granite off the Turnberry coast, and the Isle of Arran, usually cloaked in a blue-grey haze, shone green in the crisp morning air from the heights by the gleaming white Turnberry Hotel.

The wind had veered to the northwest, creating different clubbing decisions. The holes that had played downwind on Thursday played into the breeze on Friday. The seventh, for example, the 528-yard par 5 whose last 270 yards or so run uphill, had been easily reachable with medium irons during the first round, but with the shift in the wind, it called for much stronger clubbing on Friday.

The shifting wind seemed to promote better scoring, for now the home nine played with the breeze at the players' backs. Where 30 men had broken 70 in the first round, 47 shot in the 60s in the second. They were led by Mark Brooks, a Texan, who shot 64 and climbed into a tie for 13th place where only a day earlier he had faced elimination following an opening round of 74. Three others shot 65, six more shot 66, seven shot 67, 10 shot 68, and 20 shot 69. As a whole the field averaged 71.71 strokes, a little less than two over par.

At the end of the day, Watson led after an inspired round of 65 that had everyone smiling; Parnevik, the Swede, and Faxon, an American, shared second place just one stroke behind; and Price had climbed into solid contention and stood in fourth place, another stroke further back. Watson had 133 for the 36 holes, seven under par, Faxon and Parnevik had 134, and Price had 135. Greg Norman raised himself within reach of the top with a blistering birdie-birdie finish that saved a 67 and gave him 138. Now he stood five strokes behind Watson. Norman is capable of shooting any score at all, and so all five

Jesper Parnevik felt he had struggled with his opening 68, but was 'very happy' with 66 in the second round.

Nick Price (135) was inspired by two successive birdies.

Brad Faxon (134) didn't have a bogey in his 65.

strokes meant nothing with 36 holes still to play.

As one of the early starters, Brooks showed everyone what could be expected from this assemblage of the game's best players. Off at 7.55 in the fourth group of the day, along with Tom Kite and David Gilford, Brooks birdied three of the first seven holes, one of them playing downwind and two directly into the wind. Where the game's leading players had been playing wooden clubs into the third only a day earlier, Brooks had nothing but a five iron for his second, and even then he hit a rather ordinary sort of shot that ran perhaps 45 feet from the hole. But Mark ran it home and wrote a 3 on his scorecard.

Turning around now for the long run into the breeze, Brooks drilled a five iron within eight feet and birdied the fifth, holed an 18-inch putt to save his par 3 on the sixth, and followed with a 60-yard pitch to four feet for another birdie on the seventh.

Out in 32, every hole had been an adventure. In addition to his three birdies, Brooks had saved his pars on the fourth, sixth and eighth with a combination of deft chipping and inspired putting. Over the six holes from the third through the eighth he had taken only one putt on each green.

Starting back, Brooks holed from 18 feet on the 10th, missed another birdie opportunity from 14 feet on the 11th, and ripped a four iron within 15 feet on the 12th and ran another putt home. Now he had one-putted eight of 10 greens.

He would hole only once more, running in a 10-foot putt on the 16th for his final birdie of the day. Back in 32, he had shot his 64, just one stroke above the lowest round ever in an Open Championship.

While Brooks was driving scoring to lower levels, Daly, playing only a hole behind, had turned a highly promising beginning into a disappointment. Two under par as the round began, Daly had played some inspired golf on the outward nine. Three birdies had dropped him to five under par after 27 holes, but at the same time he had missed a number of opportunities that, had putts fallen from inside 15 feet, might have sent his scoring into the 20s. Then it all ended.

Out in 32, he stood on the 10th tee, wound himself into his springlike backswing that generates so much power, and played a dreadful hook that plunged

Mark Brooks (64–138) was one off the Open record.

Frank Nobilo (136) hit his irons very well.

45

First-round leader Greg Turner (136) 'had to struggle a bit' while shooting 71.

After a shaky start, Ronan Rafferty (137) settled down.

among the rocks and crevices of the beach. Swarms of spectators, officials, players and caddies searched among the debris, but no one found the ball. Daly dropped another where the original shot had crossed into the hazard, but now he stood so far back even he couldn't reach the green. On with his fourth shot, he compounded his original mistake by three-putting. He had scored 7 on a par-4 hole and wiped out all the good work he had done on the outward nine.

Worse was coming. A nice pitch on to the 11th left Daly just 20 feet from the cup, but he ran his first putt three feet past and then lipped out his second. He still had about two feet of putt left, but a comfortable stance would have put him on Vijay Singh's line of putt. Instead, Daly took an awkward stance, balanced himself on the toe of his right foot, reached across with his putter, and missed again. On in one, down in four — a double-bogey 5. Five shots thrown away on two holes. Daly was done for. He played the next seven holes in one under par, came back in 40, and shot 72 for his round. His 36-hole total of 140 qualified easily for the last two rounds, but Daly played no further part in the outcome. Reaching the sanctuary of the clubhouse, he climbed into his car and drove off saying, 'I'm going home and pull the knife out of my heart.'

Meantime, Greg Turner had run on hard times as well, but he didn't fall as far. He did, in fact, look as if he might keep up his early form when he birdied both the fourth and the difficult sixth, the long par 3 that stretches 222 yards. A six iron to six feet set up his birdie on the fourth, and he played an even better shot into the sixth, a one iron that pulled up within five feet of the cup.

When he holed that putt he stood seven under par for 24 holes, not a bad beginning at all, and he led the field. He seemed certain to fall to at least eight under par when he reached the seventh green with a three wood for his second shot, but it all ended there. Just 20 feet from the hole, Turner ran his first putt six feet past and missed. Three putts earned him no better than a par 5, and he lost three strokes over the next two holes and finished the round in 71. Turner was out of it.

Fuzzy Zoeller (137) birdied all the par-3 holes.

A second 68 put David Edwards (136) among the leaders.

Amateur Warren Bennett (139) made the 36-hole cut.

David Feherty (137) was troubled by his driving.

Barry Lane (145) holed-in-one at the fourth.

Jonathan Lomas, who had begun the day one stroke behind Turner, played the steadier round, level-par 70, but that wasn't good enough on a day like this when so many played under par.

Still, the day belonged to Watson, who was fighting to win his sixth Open Championship, which would place him alongside Harry Vardon, the only man so far to have won six. As it was, Watson stood among J.H. Taylor and James Braid from Vardon's time, and Peter Thomson, the Australian master of links golf, who won five between 1954 and 1965. Watson won his first in 1975 and his last in 1983. He might have won a sixth in 1984 had not a two iron into the 17th green at St Andrews slipped to his right, barely missed the green, and ended across the road and almost against a stone wall. The slight miss there and an earlier unplayable lie on the 12th allowed Seve Ballesteros to pass him and win his second Open.

Watson would make no mistakes except to bogey the sixth and 13th. He played as he had in his best years. The putts that hadn't fallen fell, his irons were as crisp and decisive as he had ever played them, and his driving, although not always straight, sailed long and mostly true. He began by holing two sizeable putts, one from 20 feet on the first and another from an outrageous 50 feet or more on the third.

One stroke slipped away when he missed the sixth green, but then he played five wonderful holes that combined impeccable ball-striking with the kind of nerveless putting he hadn't shown in years.

It began with the seventh, a hole where others had trouble reaching the green. After a drive just off the right of centre, Watson played his metal driver once more and drilled a low-flying shot that knifed through the wind, hit short of the green, bounded up the hill, and ran perhaps 40 feet from the cup. Two putts and he had his birdie.

His drive on the eighth, again facing into the wind, drifted into the right rough, leaving him a difficult second shot. His ball sat above his feet in a classic hook lie, but Watson ripped a three iron that settled on the green about eight feet to the right of the hole. It was a display of virtuoso shot-making that raised cheers from his growing gallery.

Now Watson stood three under par for the round and five under par for 26 holes. He played a routine par 4 at the ninth, which took him out in 32, and then moved to the 10th. Another pushed drive cost him nothing and left him a nine iron to the green. With the wind coming in from left to right and the hole cut in the front left of the green, his approach left him very little room for error. Watson started the ball directly at the flagstick. If he had gauged the distance properly, he would be in no trouble even if the wind died. Instead, it kept up its steady strength, his ball drifted slightly right and more on to the green, and pulled up about 15 feet from the cup. The putt fell, and Tom had his fifth birdie in 10 holes.

Now for the 11th, a par 3 of 177 yards. Watson played a stunning eight iron that covered the flagstick all the way and settled just four feet beyond the hole. The putt dropped, and he went to six under par. He would go no lower. A pitch to the centre of the 13th, where the pin sat on the right, cost him three putts (his second missed from no more than two feet), but he made up the stroke on the 17th, where a two-iron second shot reached the green. Two putts from 30 feet earned him his final birdie of the day.

His gallery had grown with every hole, and now it lined the last fairway, where he had won so much glory 17 years earlier. As he had then, he drove with a one iron, but where he had needed only a seven iron in 1977, he played a six iron on to the green.

Jonathan Lomas (136) was level par in the second round.

Nick Faldo (141) came back with 66.

Tommy Nakajima (141) recovered from an opening 73.

Vijay Singh (138) got under par with 68.

Greg Kraft's (143) putter was lost, but later recovered.

As he walked down the final yards through the valley created by the high grandstands, the spectators rose and applauded. Watson took off his cap and smiled.

Watson made his par, then walked off, still smiling, the gallery still cheering. Facing the Press a few minutes later, he grinned and crowed, 'Not bad for a 44-year-old has-been.'

Meanwhile, the 36-hole cut fell at 143, just three over par for Turnberry, and caught quite a few prominent players. Jack Nicklaus shot 72-73–145 and would not be around any longer, Gary Player missed, and so did Lee Trevino and Bob Charles, other great old champions. Those missing the cut also included Ian Baker-Finch, who hadn't been the same since he won at Royal Birkdale three years earlier; Payne Stewart; Gabriel Hjerstedt, a young Swede who played the first 12 holes in four under par and the remaining 24 in 11 over; Chip Beck; Corey Pavin, who played such marvellous golf against Faldo in the Toyota World Match Play Championship the previ-

Ian Woosnam (152) missed the cut by nine strokes.

Corey Pavin (151) shot 75 and 76.

Ben Crenshaw (143) barely qualified.

ous October; Scottish favourite Sam Torrance and, of course, Ian Woosnam and Phil Mickelson, who had been crippled by their opening rounds.

The championship also lost the two Amateur champions, Lee James, the British champion, and John Harris, the United States champion; but with 139 at the halfway point following a round of 67, Warren Bennett, a 22-year-old English amateur of great promise, remained in the field.

That, of course, leaves Magee, who stood so close to the top after the first round. Magee had a horrible day. Over the nine holes from the eighth through the 15th, he bogeyed eight holes, six of them in succession, beginning with the 11th. Magee didn't seem to quit, though, and fought through to the end. He finished with a birdie at the 18th and shot 80, a difference of 13 strokes over his opening 67.

After playing through the drizzly first day, Magee admitted he hadn't come to Scotland for the weather, and now he was leaving just as it was about to turn for the better.

SECOND ROUND RESULTS

HOLE	1	2	3	4	5	6	7	8	9	10	11	12	13	14	15	16	17	18	
PAR	4	4	4	3	4	3	5	4	4	4	3	4	4	4	3	4	5	4	TOTAL
Tom Watson	3	4	3	3	4	4	4	3	4	3	2	4	5	4	3	4	4	4	65-133
Jesper Parnevik	4	4	4	2	4	4	3	5	4	4	3	4	4	4	2	3	4	4	66-134
Brad Faxon	4	4	4	2	4	3	4	4	3	4	3	4	4	4	2	4	4	4	65-134
Nick Price	3	4	3	4	4	2	4	5	4	4	3	4	3	4	3	3	4	5	66-135
Greg Turner	4	4	4	2	4	2	5	6	5	3	4	4	4	4	3	4	5	4	71-136
Frank Nobilo	3	4	4	3	3	3	5	4	4	4	2	4	4	5	3	4	4	4	67-136
David Edwards	5	4	3	3	4	3	5	3	4	4	2	5	4	4	3	4	4	4	68-136
Jonathan Lomas	4	4	4	2	4	3	6	4	4	4	3	4	4	5	3	4	4	4	70-136
Fuzzy Zoeller	4	4	4	2	5	2	4	4	4	4	2	4	5	4	2	4	4	4	66-137
David Feherty	4	4	4	2	4	3	4	4	4	4	3	5	4	4	4	4	4	4	69-137
Loren Roberts	4	4	4	3	4	3	5	4	4	4	3	5	4	4	3	3	4	4	69-137
Ronan Rafferty	4	4	4	3	4	3	4	4	3	4	2	5	3	4	3	4	4	4	66-137

HOLE SUMMARY

HOLE	PAR	EAGLES	BIRDIES	PARS	BOGEYS	HIGHER	RANK	AVERAGE
1	4	0	24	114	17	1	13	3.97
2	4	0	5	104	46	1	5	4.28
3	4	0	28	99	28	1	12	4.01
4	3	1	33	105	17	0	16	2.88
5	4	0	12	94	43	7	4	4.29
6	3	0	14	75	54	13	1	3.43
7	5	1	44	88	19	4	15	4.88
8	4	0	10	75	61	10	3	4.46
9	4	0	13	110	30	3	9	4.15
OUT	35	2	183	864	315	40		36.35
10	4	0	14	108	30	4	8	4.16
11	3	0	38	105	12	1	17	2.85
12	4	1	10	95	48	2	6	4.26
13	4	0	23	95	35	3	10	4.12
14	4	0	7	73	67	9	2	4.51
15	3	0	15	105	31	5	7	3.18
16	4	0	37	99	14	6	14	3.93
17	5	8	92	54	2	0	18	4.32
18	4	0	28	100	25	3	11	4.03
IN	35	9	264	834	264	33		35.36
TOTAL	70	11	447	1698	579	73		71.71

Players Below Par		47
Players At Par		15
Players Above Par		94

LOW SCORES

Low First Nine	Terry Price	31
Low Second Nine	Mark James	31
Low Round	Mark Brooks	64

There is something for everyone in the Golf Exhibition at the Open Championship.

53

Jesper Parnevik was best known for his unusual headwear until his strong performance in the Open Championship.

SWEDISH GOLF COMES OF AGE

BY MARINO PARASCENZO

Take one look at Jesper Parnevik and you want to give him some money and tell him to buy an ice cream cone. He is baby-faced and all wide-eyed and wonder, wearing the bill of his golf cap turned up, as though he were skating into a stiff wind. A froth of light brown hair curls up from underneath, right where the cap meets his forehead. Don't let impressions fool you. You're looking at the future of Swedish golf, maybe even of European golf. And not just in Parnevik.

The question used to be, who would be the first Swede to win on the PGA European Tour? Ove Sellberg answered that in the 1986 Epson Grand Prix of Europe, a match-play event. The first Swede to

Swedish star Per-Ulrik Johansson.

play in the Ryder Cup? Answer: Joakim Haeggman in 1993. Now the question is, who will be the first Swede to win the Open Championship?

Parnevik, 29, came within a whisker of answering it at Turnberry. History will note that Parnevik, playing in a vacuum of his own making, didn't realize he was leading, feared he needed a birdie at the 18th hole and, in gambling for that birdie, made a bogey that proved fatal to his chances.

His second-place finish was the best ever by a Swede in the Open Championship, bettering Robert Karlsson's tie for fifth place in 1992 at Muirfield. In the process, Parnevik upstaged another Swede, Anders Forsbrand, and thrilled millions watching on television round the world, and especially those in Sweden.

You don't have to go back very far to get a sense of how far the Swedes have come in golf. It's so common to see Swedes in the field that you tend to doubt

the records. Could it be that in Turnberry's first Open 17 years ago, there was only one in the championship, Gunnar Mueller?

In 1980, there were none. In 1981, there was Tore Sviland, an amateur, and in 1982 there were two amateurs, Magnus Persson and Per Andersson, both of whom would later become professionals. Then that vigorous Swedish junior programme began to bear fruit. In 1985, at Royal St George's, three Swedes made the 36-hole cut — Forsbrand, Sellberg and Persson — and two others qualified, for a total of five in the championship.

And so it has gone over the brief, rapid years until 1994, when two Swedes might have won the Open Championship. Forsbrand put on a furious charge the final day, one stroke off the Open record with 64, to tie for fourth place. Twenty Swedes were in the final qualifying for this year's Open, the third most outside the home countries. Six of those qualified, for a total of 10 Swedes in the championship.

Ten years ago, there were eight Swedes on the PGA European Tour, and now there are about two dozen. The Order of Merit after the Open Championship listed 13 Swedes in the top 100 and eight in the top 50, led by Forsbrand in the 11th position. The others were Parnevik, Haeggman, Karlsson, Gabriel Hjerstedt, Peter Hedblom, Per-Ulrik Johansson and Mats Lanner.

At the same time, five Swedes were to be found in the top 100 of the Sony Ranking, led by Parnevik, ranked No. 37 in the world. Also listed were Haeggman, Forsbrand, Johansson and Karlsson.

The topic of Swedish golf was raised in the pre-

Gabriel Hjertstedt had been among the year's leaders.

Joakim Haeggman was the first Swede in the Ryder Cup.

championship Press conference with Greg Norman, the defending champion. 'There are a lot of good quality players and one is going to win a major, whether this week, next or whenever,' Norman said. 'You have to take a kid out and groom him. It is a 10-year process. It doesn't happen in two or three years. The Swedish Federation understands that, and has been most successful in doing that.'

In comparison to the Swedes, the success of the Spaniards and Germans seems largely unplanned by any federation, which it was. Seve Ballesteros, Jose Maria Olazabal and Bernhard Langer were lone wolves in that sense, and their rise to world prominence in golf was due almost entirely to their own ability and desire.

As with tennis in a previous generation, the Swedes approached golf with a team concept; in other words, a support system. Most probably would not reach the heights of the game, but the odds were improved for the most talented and determined few.

'It is very cheap to play golf in Sweden so long as you are a junior,' Parnevik said. 'It costs maybe £50 if you are under 21. That gives you membership and free practice with a local pro. From ages eight to 14, they have a tournament during the summer, with qualifying from regional events. Ages 15 and 16, you can join the Team Tour, and play every week on different courses in Sweden.'

The Swedish Federation has supported the most promising golfers on into the PGA European Tour. Sellberg's historic first victory in 1986 was followed in 1987 by Lanner's win in the same Epson Grand Prix and, later that year, by Forsbrand's triumph in a stroke-play event, the Ebel European Masters-Swiss Open.

Forsbrand, 33, has been Sweden's most successful professional so far, and his victory in the 1994 Moroccan Open was the seventh of his career. The week before, Lanner won the Maderia Island Open, giving the Swedes victories in the first two PGA European Tour events of the year. Haeggman also won early in 1994, in the Benson & Hedges Malaysian Open.

For a further point of reference in Swedish golf, go back only two years to the 1992 US Masters. Forsbrand, who had led Sweden to victories in the 1991 Alfred Dunhill Cup and World Cup, was there only as a television commentator. He returned to the Masters as a contestant in 1993, and tied for 11th place.

And many people thought Spain was the emerging nation in European golf. Three Spaniards played all four rounds in the Open Championship — Ballesteros, Olazabal and Domingo Hospital — and they tied for 38th place. The Swedes don't yet have a dominating figure like Ballesteros or Olazabal, but they have depth. Five Swedes played all 72 holes in this Open. Following Parnevik and Forsbrand were Lanner, tied for 51st; Johansson, the 1991 Rookie of the Year and a teammate of Forsbrand in the two 1991 team titles, tied for 60th; and Haeggman, who was a distant joint 76th.

But Haeggman already had this distinction — the first Swede to play in the Ryder Cup. Haeggman scored his first victory in the 1993 Peugeot Open de Espana. 'If people haven't mentioned my name with the Ryder Cup,' he said, 'then maybe it's time they did.' He was chosen by captain Bernard Gallacher for the 1993 match at The Belfry. He and Olazabal were beaten by Raymond Floyd and Payne Stewart in the second-day fourballs, but he paid that back with a singles victory over John Cook.

Not surprisingly, along the way some of the Swedes found golf's Northwest Passage. American collegiate golf is the next step up from the Swedish Federation programme. Johansson played at Arizona State University when that team, including Phil Mickelson, won the 1990 NCAA Championship.

Swedish women, some also following the trail to American colleges, have not come out in as large numbers as the men, but in several instances have achieved even greater success, including two major championships on the American LPGA Tour. Liselotte Neumann won the 1988 US Women's Open and Helen Alfredsson won the 1993 Nabisco Dinah Shore. By the summer, both already had victories in 1994. Annika Sorenstam, the 1991 College Player of the Year at the University of Arizona, joined the LPGA Tour this year after having four second-place finishes on the 1993 European women's circuit.

Parnevik took up golf when he was aged eight and within five years had stated his intention to win the Open Championship. After progressing through the Swedish junior programme, Parnevik played from 1984 to 1986 at Palm Beach Junior College in Florida, then qualified for the PGA European Tour in 1987. He did not place higher than 48th on the Order of Merit until 1993, when he won the Bell's Scottish Open by five strokes. He finished 17th on the 1993 Order of Merit, then qualified for the PGA Tour in America. He was 79th on their money list before the Open Championship.

Anders Forsbrand has been Sweden's most successful golfer.

Parnevik, although soft-spoken, has been regarded as a highly-driven man. He developed an ulcer in his first full year on the European Tour. He also was still learning to cope with the pressure of having a famous name. His father, Bo, is Sweden's most famous comedian and impersonator. 'I could win the Grand Slam,' Jesper said earlier this year, smiling, 'and still not be the most famous Parnevik in Sweden.'

In golf, Parnevik was best known for the unusual manner in which he wore his golf cap, with the bill turned up. He began doing that in Florida several years ago, so he could get a better tan on his face. 'I found I could putt better that way,' Parnevik said. 'I could see better. The bill didn't get in my way. So I left it turned up.' The only problem was, the logo on Parnevik's cap was obscured, but Titleist solved that by embroidering on the underside of the bill.

Partly because of the way he wore his cap, Parnevik may not have had the respect as a golfer that he came to earn at Turnberry. 'Jesper showed me a lot of soul,' said Tom Watson, who played alongside Parnevik in the last two rounds. 'He's a good strong player who doesn't let anything distract him. He's going to win a lot of tournaments.'

'You have youth on your side,' champion Nick Price, who suffered heartbreaking losses in the 1982 and 1988 Opens, told Parnevik at the trophy ceremony. 'I hope you'll use it wisely.'

Fuzzy Zoeller (201) shot 64 and birdied four of the last seven holes.

3

SIX ARE WITHIN ONE STROKE

BY ROBERT SOMMERS

Watching Fuzzy Zoeller play golf is watching a man who seems to be at peace with himself. He walks with an unhurried gait, although he plays his shots quickly with a minimum of fuss, occasionally shares a quip with the gallery, and when he's not talking he's whistling, not always a recognisable tune but surely something that quiets a racing heartbeat, for he can't always be as placid as he appears.

There have been few others like him. Julius Boros comes to mind, another placid, often phlegmatic golfer of great ability. Like Zoeller, Boros had been known to sling a club across his shoulder and whistle after botching a shot in a tense moment. No one, though, can remember seeing Boros wave the white flag of surrender.

Our most enduring and endearing memory of Zoeller must be the moment when Greg Norman holed the putt from across the 18th green at Winged Foot, and Zoeller assumed Norman had won the 1984 United States Open Championship. Seeing the putt fall from his position down the fairway, Zoeller snatched his towel from off his golf bag and waved it overhead, believing Norman had beaten him. He hadn't. Norman had wasted a stroke by hitting his approach shot into a grandstand and had needed that putt not to win but to tie Fuzzy. The next day Zoeller played an impeccable 67 and beat Norman by eight strokes in the play-off.

It was difficult to believe that 10 years had passed

Larry Mize (206) moved up with 64.

since that Sunday, especially watching Zoeller tear around Turnberry in 64 strokes in the Open's third round, climb over seven other players, and claim a share of first place, at 201, along with Brad Faxon, another American. To move into such a commanding position, Zoeller had played the last 36 holes in 130 strokes, following his second round of 66.

Faxon, meanwhile, shot 67 to go with his 65 of the previous day.

Zoeller's was, of course, the low score of the day, but he wasn't alone. He was matched by Larry Mize, who had barely qualified for the last two rounds after a 73-69 start.

Once again we had a day of strikingly low scoring. Of the 81 players who had qualified for the last two rounds, 42 men, better than half the field, shot in the 60s. Besides Zoeller and Mize at 64, Ronan Rafferty and Colin Montgomerie shot 65s, nine others shot 66s, eight more shot 67, seven shot 68, and 14 men shot 69.

Tom Watson was among those at 69. By then he had played three rounds in the 60s and suddenly found himself in third place, at 202, tied with three others. Rafferty had caught him, and so had Nick Price, with his 67, and Jesper Parnevik with 68. David Feherty, the whimsical and impulsive Irishman, shot 66 and climbed into a threatening position at 203.

From the scores it is easy to conclude that

Irish interest was high as David Feherty (203, top) and Ronan Rafferty (202, bottom) were within two of the lead.

Turnberry was at its least forbidding. The cold wind from the west had calmed to little more than a fresh breeze, the sun wiped away the overcast, the sun sparkled on the Clyde, and sailing craft rode the fresh breeze from off shore.

It was a day made for low scoring. Temperatures climbed once again, and the greens, still soft from weekend rains, remained inviting, ideal for target golf. Players could throw their shots directly at the flagsticks with little need to play the low, running shots common to links golf.

The conditions were reflected by the results of the day's play as first one man and then another made his run at the leaders. Watson found himself under siege from the start. Greg Norman had begun his third round almost an hour and a half before Watson by birdieing two of the first three holes and giving every indication he was off to one of his extraordinary rounds.

Another birdie on the ninth and he had gone out in 32, but he could make up no further ground coming home, and then threw it all away on the 16th. A too-finely gauged pitch just missed carrying to the green, caught the top of the bank that falls away into a tiny stream below, and tumbled into the water. Norman lost two strokes to par, and his defense of his cham-

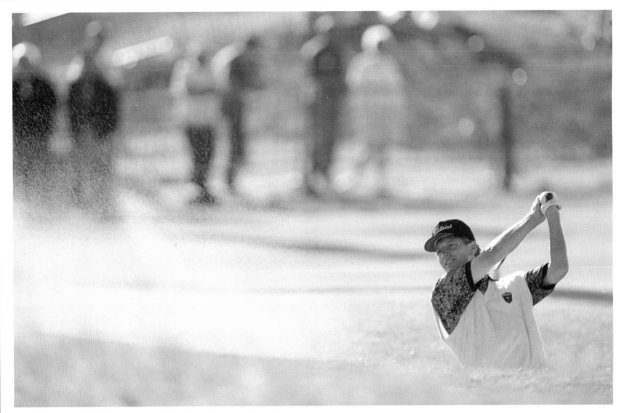

Brad Faxon (201) had gone 41 holes without dropping a shot to par.

pionship had ended.

Zoeller, meanwhile, starting just 40 minutes before Watson and Parnevik, was off to a much slower start. A birdie on the first was wiped out by a bogey 5 on the fifth.

As Watson and Parnevik were both taking standard par 4s on the first, Faxon, just ahead of them, birdied the second, rolling in a putt from 35 feet. Six under par as the round began, Faxon had dropped to seven under and caught Watson.

Two holes later Watson surged ahead again. His seven-iron approach had bounced over the third green and into the rough, but Watson had never been uncomfortable with the little pitch shot. He lined it up, dug the ball out of the grass, and watched as it rolled 40 feet toward the flagstick. Just as it had 14 years earlier in the US Open at Pebble Beach, Watson's ball ran to the edge of the hole and wedged itself between the flagstick and the lip of the cup. He had birdied.

Eight under par now, Watson had moved ahead once more, while visions of Pebble Beach and his victory over Jack Nicklaus surfaced once again. Sadly for Watson and his loyalists, he would make no more headway. He gave that stroke away with a badly misplayed six iron to the fourth that curled left

A bogey at the 18th put Nick Price (202) one stroke behind.

Jesper Parnevik (202) bogeyed two of the first six holes, but found his swing before the turn and shot 32 on the second nine.

and settled in high grass on the steep bank along the green's left side. Watson took three strokes to get down and fell back to seven under par once again.

Now Watson was tied with Faxon, with Rafferty, making an early run, six under par after the seventh, tied with Price and Parnevik. Norman and Greg Turner, the first-round leader, stood another two strokes behind at five under par. Neither Turner nor Norman would play a further part in contending for the Open title, but Feherty had picked up one stroke by birdieing the fifth, and at four under par had closed within three strokes of the lead.

Price, meantime, had birdied the seventh and drawn even at seven under par after the shakiest of starts. He had pounded a very long drive on the first hole, which played downwind, but if his ball lay 90 yards short of the green, his pitch didn't carry 25. It was an awful looking shot, but Price had the luckiest kind of break. His ball carried just far enough to catch a downslope on the fairway, then bounced and rolled perhaps 10 or 12 yards short of the green. His pitch was not a thing of beauty, either; it ran so far past the hole he was still outside Faxon. A dangerous player when his putter is working, Price saved himself by rolling in the 12-foot putt.

He birdied the seventh with a pitch to two feet,

and now he stood tied with both Watson and Faxon at seven under par for 43 holes.

Moments later, Watson came to the seventh and, as he had done on Friday, he ripped into two drivers and two-putted for his third consecutive birdie on this hole. Once again he moved ahead at eight under par, but his time was running out.

Meanwhile, up ahead, Zoeller had begun his march. After missing a four-foot putt that cost him the bogey on the fifth, Fuzzy drilled a three wood into the wind on the sixth and rolled in a 20-foot putt with a five-foot break and followed by nearly holing a little pitch to the seventh and holing from inside a foot. Now he stood at two under par for the round, and when he parred the next two holes he had gone out in 33. At five under par for 45 holes, he was still three strokes behind Watson, and two behind Faxon and Price.

Now Zoeller was about to begin his final spurt home while others closed in on Watson.

As it had on Friday, the wind, although lighter, helped on the second nine, where most of those who rode to the top made their birdies. Rafferty was the exception. Playing just ahead of Zoeller and Feherty, Rafferty had birdied both the first and fourth, the 167-yard par 3, with two precise irons, and then

62

Loren Roberts (206) had a third under-par score.

Tom Watson (202) had an erratic putting round.

Greg Turner (206) remained a contender.

Davis Love III (206) shot 68 to share ninth place.

It was a beautiful Scottish afternoon for sailing and golf, as David Feherty teed off on the ninth hole.

Tsukasa Watanabe (211) joined the low scoring with 68.

threw away a stroke on the fifth, which, at 441 yards into the wind, had turned into the most difficult hole on the course that day.

A drive with a three wood and then a four iron that drifted into the rough cost him a 5, but Rafferty turned his game around on the next two holes. Putting as he hadn't done in more than a year, Ronan holed from 25 feet on the sixth, and followed by holing from six feet on the seventh. Out in 32 he had gone to six under par. With Watson still at eight under, Rafferty stood within two strokes of the lead. He would never be farther behind the rest of the afternoon, and indeed would be closer.

While Watson could hardly be said to struggle, he could make nothing on the greens, although he had a number of opportunities. He played the first nine in 34, but with the way the rest of the leaders were scoring, he would need something better than that.

Zoeller, meantime, played a series of undistinguished irons to 25 feet on the 12th and to 20 feet on the 13th, but a hot putter covers many sins, and here he began holing putts. Both fell, and now he stood at

Peter Senior (206) had 67, his best score.

Mark Calcavecchia (208) shot 31 on the second nine for 67.

seven under par, within one stroke of Watson and tied with both Price, who had gone out in 33, and Faxon, who had shot 34.

Just about then Faxon showed why he is considered among the best putters in the game. A rather loose approach left him 30 feet from the cup on the 10th, but he ran his putt home for the birdie, and now he had climbed into a tie with Watson at eight under par. Price and Zoeller stood a stroke behind them, and Rafferty a further stroke back.

The race remained tight the rest of the afternoon with Zoeller continuing his relentless drive to a share of the lead position, Rafferty and Feherty picking up a further stroke each, Parnevik coming back from some grim moments, and Watson first giving signs he would yield, and then once again coming back to challenge.

Zoeller played both the 14th and 15th safely, and then lofted a soft pitching wedge within 10 feet on the 16th and holed the putt. Eight under par now, tied with Watson and Faxon, one stroke ahead of Price, Parnevik and Rafferty — six men within one

stroke of one another.

Now all kinds of changes were taking place. Parnevik misjudged his approach to the 13th badly, left his pitch short and bogeyed; and then Watson, who had holed a series of nerve-wracking putts, rammed his 30-foot approach putt perhaps five feet past and three-putted the 14th. He fell to seven under par, one stroke off the lead now.

Minutes earlier both Price and Faxon had bunkered their approaches to the 14th, but both men had dug out of the sand within reasonable distance of the cup and holed their putts to save pars.

At about that time Zoeller two-putted from 25 feet on the 17th and birdied. Now he stood alone at nine under par, one stroke ahead of the field. By then as well, Rafferty had holed from 15 feet on the 18th and gone to eight under par. What had been a fluid situation had become liquid. No one could be sure exactly what was happening.

Watson lost another stroke on the 16th, where he three-putted once more, again leaving himself a putt of four or five feet. Just as it had on the 14th, his

Wayne Grady (209) matched the low on the second nine.

second putt actually hit the inside of the hole but turned away to the left and sat inches from the cup. With that he fell to six under par, three strokes off Zoeller's score.

This was turning into a grim afternoon for Watson. The crowd clearly pulled for him to play well — indeed to win — and he was playing his shots as well as he ever had, but somehow he couldn't score. Both putts he missed at such cost had been struck well enough, and had looked at first as if they would surely drop, but each had refused.

He had holed a few of those already, one from a bit longer to save par on the 12th, and his putt from 20 feet or more on the 11th had run directly at the hole but pulled up within two inches of falling.

Watson, though, is nothing if not a fighter. He wasn't through yet.

Zoeller, meanwhile, had played the 18th as it was meant to be played. His drive ended in the absolute centre of the fairway, and with the hole cut toward the right rear of the green, his pitch hit, bounced once, then braked no more than 10 feet to the right of the cup, hole high.

He was already six under par for the round; a birdie here would tie the Open record of 63. He took care lining up his putt and stroked it nicely, but he had misread the line. He had expected his ball to curl left toward the cup, but it rolled straight. Neverthe-

less, he was in with 64 and had his 201 total.

This was a wonderful pairing to watch, for Feherty had matched him almost stroke for stroke with his 66, and stood just two strokes back at 203.

With those two finished, along with Rafferty, only two more pairings mattered. Faxon and Price had come off the 16th green at eight under par, and then both birdied the 17th, pulling even with Zoeller with only the home hole left. Price's tee shot with a two iron drifted into the right rough, but Faxon had worse luck. He pulled his two iron slightly into a steep-walled fairway bunker and had no chance to play for the green. Instead he pitched back on to the fairway and followed with a stunning iron that dug in five feet left of the cup.

Meantime, Price's pitch came out with no backspin on it. It hit toward the front of the green and raced all the way across into the rough beyond. His chip pulled up short by nine feet, and he missed his putt. Even with the closing bogey Nick shot 67, but he had given away a stroke, and when Faxon holed his putt, Price stood a stroke behind both Brad and Fuzzy.

Now Watson and Parnevik came to the closing hole.

Where Watson had bogeyed the 16th, Parnevik had birdied and passed him, at seven under against Watson's six under.

Now Watson showed his fighting spirit. After a three wood from the 17th tee, he played a marvellous two iron that carried to the top of the hill, ran on to the green, and rolled dead within holing distance of an eagle 3, perhaps 15 feet from the cup.

Parnevik, meanwhile, had reached the green with his second shot as well, but struggled to get down in two from 35 feet.

Watson played a very fine putt that for one heartstopping moment looked as if it might fall, but it missed. Still, Tom had his birdie, then played a one iron and a six iron on to the 18th green, and once more a putt fell, this from 10 feet. Once given up as finished, he had pulled himself back into the race and now stood only one stroke behind the co-leaders Zoeller and Faxon, tied with Price, Parnevik and Rafferty, with Feherty just one more stroke behind.

Frank Nobilo (208) stumbled to 72.

Mark McNulty (209) shot 68.

Greg Norman (207) saved par here at the fifth, but had 69 as his score was ruined at the 16th by a double bogey.

THIRD ROUND RESULTS

HOLE	1	2	3	4	5	6	7	8	9	10	11	12	13	14	15	16	17	18	
PAR	4	4	4	3	4	3	5	4	4	4	3	4	4	4	3	4	5	4	TOTAL
Fuzzy Zoeller	3	4	4	3	5	2	4	4	4	4	3	3	3	4	3	3	4	4	64-201
Brad Faxon	4	3	4	3	4	3	5	4	4	3	3	4	4	4	3	4	4	4	67-201
Ronan Rafferty	3	4	4	2	5	2	4	4	4	5	3	3	4	4	3	3	5	3	65-202
Nick Price	4	3	4	3	4	3	4	4	4	4	3	4	4	2	4	4	5	5	67-202
Jesper Parnevik	4	4	4	3	5	4	4	4	4	3	3	3	5	4	3	3	4	4	68-202
Tom Watson	4	4	3	4	4	3	4	4	4	4	3	4	4	5	3	5	4	3	69-202
David Feherty	4	4	4	3	3	3	5	4	4	3	3	4	4	4	2	4	4	4	66-203
Mark James	4	4	4	3	4	3	4	3	5	4	3	3	3	4	2	4	5	4	66-205
Larry Mize	4	4	4	2	5	3	4	4	4	4	3	4	4	4	2	3	4	3	64-206
Colin Montgomerie	3	4	4	2	5	3	4	5	3	3	3	4	4	4	3	5	5	3	65-206
Andrew Coltart	5	4	4	2	3	3	5	5	4	4	3	4	3	3	3	3	4	4	66-206
Masashi Ozaki	3	4	4	3	3	4	5	4	3	4	3	4	4	3	3	3	5	4	66-206
Tom Kite	3	4	4	4	4	3	5	4	4	4	4	3	3	3	3	4	3	4	66-206
Craig Stadler	3	4	3	3	4	4	3	3	4	4	4	4	4	4	3	4	4	4	66-206
Peter Senior	4	4	4	3	4	3	5	3	4	4	3	4	4	5	3	4	3	3	67-206
Peter Jacobsen	4	4	4	2	4	3	4	4	4	4	3	4	4	4	3	4	3	5	67-206
Davis Love III	4	4	4	2	4	3	5	4	3	4	3	4	3	5	3	4	5	4	68-206
Loren Roberts	4	4	3	4	4	2	5	5	5	3	3	4	3	4	3	4	5	4	69-206
Greg Turner	4	4	4	2	5	3	5	5	4	4	2	4	4	5	3	4	4	4	70-206

HOLE SUMMARY

HOLE	PAR	EAGLES	BIRDIES	PARS	BOGEYS	HIGHER	RANK	AVERAGE
1	4	0	20	55	5	1	16	3.84
2	4	0	10	54	16	1	4	4.10
3	4	0	16	50	14	1	8	4.00
4	3	0	18	54	9	0	15	2.89
5	4	0	5	44	27	5	1	4.41
6	3	0	8	56	15	2	2	3.14
7	5	2	29	45	3	2	17	4.68
8	4	0	10	54	17	0	5	4.09
9	4	0	6	63	12	0	6	4.07
OUT	35	2	122	475	118	12		35.22
10	4	0	10	57	14	0	7	4.05
11	3	0	12	59	8	2	8	3.00
12	4	0	15	58	7	1	13	3.93
13	4	0	11	62	7	1	10	3.98
14	4	0	8	54	18	1	3	4.15
15	3	0	13	63	5	0	14	2.90
16	4	0	17	54	6	4	12	3.96
17	5	9	45	27	0	0	18	4.22
18	4	0	15	54	11	1	10	3.98
IN	35	9	146	488	76	10		34.17
TOTAL	70	11	268	963	194	22		69.39

Players Below Par	42
Players At Par	10
Players Above Par	29

LOW SCORES

Low First Nine	Craig Stadler	31
Low Second Nine	Mark Calcavecchia	31
	Andrew Coltart	31
	Wayne Grady	31
	Tom Kite	31
	Larry Mize	31
	Fuzzy Zoeller	31
Low Round	Larry Mize	64
	Fuzzy Zoeller	64

Approximately 128,000 spectators attended the Open Championship at Turnberry.

Andrew Coltart's goal was to make the 36-hole cut in the Open Championship. He did — then shot 66 in the third round.

NO GIMMICKS, TRICKS, NONSENSE

BY ALISTER NICOL

Golf is a crazy numbers game, but one that is easy to figure out.

Winner Nick Price became only the fourth man in Open Championship history to shoot below 70 in all four rounds, and proudly walked away from the closing ceremony with a cheque for £110,000 and the old claret jug. Being owner for a year of the most prized trophy in world golf will bring further, almost incalculable riches to the 37-year-old who was born in South Africa, plays for Zimbabwe, lives in Florida and travels on a British passport.

The third man in history to card all four rounds in the 60s was Jesper Parnevik. The Swede stood on the 18th tee in the final round with a three-shot lead over Price, bogeyed the hole and succumbed to a birdie, eagle, par finish by his eventual conqueror. Parnevik tucked a cheque for £88,000 in his wallet. Like Price, he went through the 72 holes with nothing uglier than 5 on each of his four scorecards.

In stark contrast, John Daly, arguably the biggest name in the Royal and Ancient game, although all-too frequently for the wrong reasons, finished last of the 81 qualifiers. That was due almost entirely to his inability to avoid what Unisys, the official Open Championship scoring system, described as 'disasters.' His cash reward was, in his terms, a paltry £3,500.

The Ailsa course was not tricked up in any way. It was an honest-to-goodness links course, albeit with fairways and greens softened to a greater degree than the Championship Committee of the Royal and Ancient Golf Club would have wished by more than an

Masashi Ozaki shot a third-round 66.

inch of rainfall in the days preceding the championship.

Like all links courses — and the R and A will never, I trust, take the Open inland — the Ailsa's only true defence is a strong wind. The Old Course at St Andrews, Muirfield, Royal Troon, Royal Lytham, Royal Birkdale, right down to Royal St George's on the shores of the English Channel, they are all the same.

Without a good wind, not a 15 miles-an-hour breeze but a decent blow upwards of 25 miles an hour, their defences are down. They are all wide open to the highly skilled, workaholic predators of modern golf. Today's top players gobble up all the assistance offered them by the leaps and bounds in technology in this space age. Then they work like demons to make the fullest use of every advantage offered.

When they arrive at an Open Championship they find a venue honestly prepared and presented. No gimmicks, no tricks, no nonsense. Their examination is laid out before them.

That is not always the case in championship golf. The United States Golf Association, the R and A's American equivalent, have earned the unenviable reputation as golf's Torquemada, 15th Century Spain's first inquisitor-general. Oakmont this year was a prime example of the way they set up courses so penal that contenders write themselves off almost before a ball has been struck.

Almost any errant tee shot which misses a manicured fairway finds rough often so thick that wrist damage is a distinct possibility in trying to free the ball. Greens have collars of clinging thick rough out of which even the most skilled of players have diffi-

Mark James finished with three rounds in the 60s.

Craig Stadler described Turnberry as 'vulnerable.'

culty finding control of their golf ball.

And the greens are frequently lightning quick.

The USGA claim they are merely trying to identify the best player round that particular course that particular week. Their definition of the best seems to me to be a narrow one. They want their champion to be a robot-like creature who monotonously hits every fairway and every green in exactly the right spot — then putts like a dream.

There is a great deal of merit in that credo. Any player who can do exactly what the USGA demand he do has to be one heck of a golfer. But so much of the USGA's course preparation is needlessly artificial. They seem to go out of their way to prevent a rash of low scoring, such as that which made Turnberry 1994 such an exciting championship. Throughout the four days, 59 eagles and 1,298 birdies were ripped from the Ailsa course by the modern marauders of golf. There was a record of 148 rounds below 70.

Each year the US Masters at Augusta National Golf Club promises a feast of birdies and eagles because Alister Mackenzie and Bobby Jones designed the course to suit and reward attacking play. There is no rough, the fairways are generously wide and generally speaking the notorious greens, while fast and often difficult to read, are receptive to the perfectly struck iron shots which come fizzing off the clubheads of today's high-class performers.

Not so this year. For whatever reason, and I suspect I know one, this spring Augusta's greens were like marble-topped tables. Former champion Sandy Lyle hit a monstrous 355-yard drive down the long 15th, leaving himself only a wedge shot to the green. Although he may have fallen some from his once-majestic heights, the big Scot can still apply as much furious backspin on a ball as anyone. His approach to the 15th landed on the heart of the green, took one huge bounce and went clear through the back. That was unfair.

Many of Augusta's greens were like that, and Jose Maria Olazabal's victory was a tribute to his chipping and putting skills. Augusta had, like the US Open invariably does, erected artificial barriers to low scoring. I suspect they were startled into doing so by Greg Norman's phenomenal 24-under-par total a few weeks previously in The Players Championship at Sawgrass in North Florida. The Great White Shark was not the only one on the rampage that week. Former US Masters and US Open champion Fuzzy Zoeller also shattered the previous record when he plunged to 20 under par.

No one at Augusta National will, I am certain, ever admit those twin assaults on Sawgrass influenced their thinking for the 1994 US Masters in any way. Maybe it was just sheer coincidence after all. However that may be, the R and A paid no heed for the 1994 Open Championship.

Back in 1986, a wet Ayrshire spring, with constant rains driven by moisture-laden winds whipping in from the sea, produced US Open-like rough. The powers-that-be from St Andrews elected to leave it as it was, Mother Nature and all that, with only ribbon-like fairways. There were squeals of 'unfair' from some of the world's best golfers. Norman's second-round 63, en route to the first of his two Opens, was later described by Tom Watson as 'the greatest round of golf in any championship in which I have been a competitor.'

This year, a dry spring precluded an abundance of heavy rough, but the R and A strongly resisted any temptation to 'trick-up' the course. In fact several players, notably past champion Lee Trevino, claimed the Ailsa course was too easy. After missing the 36-hole cut, Trevino carped that watering systems had detracted from the true links nature of Open Championship golf. He bemoaned the idea that perfect lies took away the skill of manufacturing shots.

Championship Committee Chairman Neil Roach denied there had been over-use of Turnberry's watering system. 'It was all down to Mother Nature,' he insisted. 'In fact, course superintendent George Brown, who did a magnificent job of preparing the course, rarely used the watering system. When he did, it was only to prevent the grass from dying.'

The course record of 63 — which is the record for all four major championships — was not equalled at Turnberry, far less beaten. The best were 64s by Zoeller, Mark Brooks, Anders Forsbrand, Nick Faldo

Colin Montgomerie had two bogeys in his third-round 65.

and Larry Mize. Zoeller's was surely something of a record in its own right. It did not include a single 3, par or otherwise, but had four birdie 2s.

Generally, the scoring was incredibly good by the best players but fairly ordinary by the others; and that was I am sure because there was none of the artificiality built in by the hosts of the other major championships.

And what is wrong with low scoring? The players love it because it is a true reflection of their abundant skills, and golf watchers respond enthusiastically whether in the flesh or watching television. Low numbers are the valued currency of golf; and, in their infinite wisdom and true understanding of the game, the Royal and Ancient Golf Club will, I hope, never stoop to falsifying any of their examinations for the best players.

Secretary Michael Bonallack said, 'Low scoring does not particularly worry us so long as the best player wins. In any case, what could we possibly do to the Old Course at St Andrews next year? We would never be allowed to touch it.'

Nick Price and caddie Jeff (Squeeky) Medlen celebrated after Price's 50-foot eagle putt went in the cup on the 17th hole.

4

BOTH HANDS ON THE TROPHY

BY ROBERT SOMMERS

Perhaps there have been others as telling as the 50-foot putt that fell for Nick Price on Turnberry's 17th hole and changed the outcome of the 123rd Open Championship, but only a few come easily to mind. There was of course Bobby Jones' from 40 feet on the final green at Interlachen, in Minneapolis, that clinched the 1930 US Open, Ben Hogan's from 30 feet on the 17th at Merion that assured he would win the play-off for the 1950 US Open, Jack Nicklaus' from 40 feet on the 16th at Augusta National that won him the 1975 US Masters, Tom Watson's from about the same distance on Turnberry's 15th hole that tore the heart from Nicklaus in the 1977 Open Championship, Larry Nelson's from more than 60 feet on Oakmont's 16th hole that beat Watson in the 1983 US Open, and, of course, Hale Irwin's putt from 45 feet that broke at least five feet on the final green at Medinah, in Chicago, that forced a play-off for the 1990 US Open, which he won.

Price's heroic putt will certainly take its place among those great moments of the past. When the ball fell, Price had gained the strokes he needed if he were to realize his dream of winning the Open.

He had held it in his grasp twice before, and twice it had slipped away, first at Royal Troon 12 years earlier, when as a much less experienced young man he lost four strokes over the last five holes. Six years later, at Royal Lytham and St Annes, Price had gone into the last round leading Seve Ballesteros and Nick Faldo by two strokes, shot 69, and been passed by Ballesteros, who blistered the course with 65.

Now, at Turnberry, Price stood on the 17th tee two strokes behind Jesper Parnevik, the young Swede with the turned-up cap bill who had just birdied the 17th to move to 12 under par. When Jesper holed his putt from no more than three feet, almost everyone probably assumed he had won.

Price, however, wouldn't give up. He had just birdied the 16th, which buoyed his confidence after surviving some shaky moments through the earlier holes. Knowing what he needed, realizing he had lost two chances to win the Open already, he ripped into a driver and followed with a four iron from about 215 yards that flew over the brow of the rise leading to the green and settled on the green's left rear corner at least 50 feet from the cup.

After surveying the putt from every conceivable angle, Price gave the ball a firm rap. It rolled toward the hole, took a slight break to the right, slowed to a creeping pace, and tumbled into the cup. So truly had Nick gauged the distance, one was left with the impression that if his target had been no more than a circle drawn on the grass, his ball would have stopped inside it.

With the putt, Price went to 12 under par, which was all he needed, for by then Parnevik had misjudged his shot into the 18th and bogeyed. A safe pitch to the home green after another precisely played tee shot, then two putts and Price had won.

It was an immensely satisfying victory, for Price is among the more likeable men who play this game, and his winning had meant so much to him. He wanted to win this one badly. He did it in style, playing the last nine holes in 31, shooting 66 for the day and 268 for the 72 holes, one stroke above the record score set only a year earlier by Greg Norman. His 268 had also matched the record set over this same links course by Tom Watson in 1977.

His scoring over the last 54 holes had been phenomenal. With rounds of 66, 67 and another 66, he had shot 199, breaking a record that had stood for 17 years. When Watson beat Nicklaus in that most stirring of all Open finishes, he had played the last three rounds in 70-65-65–200. Faldo had equalled Watson's score in 1993, shooting 63-70-67–200 as he finished second to Norman at Royal St George's. It should be mentioned as well that with 66-64-70 in the last three rounds, Fuzzy Zoeller joined Watson

It was one of the longest and most significant putts in major championship history ...

... and when it fell in the hole, Price knew he was on his way to winning the Open Championship.

Jesper Parnevik missed the 15th green and bogeyed. With three birdies in the previous four holes, he still led by one.

and Faldo at the 200 level.

It had been quite a week.

Winding up his appearance before the Press after climbing into a tie for third place on the wings of a stunning 67 on Saturday, Price looked ahead to the final round and said, 'There will be no sitting about waiting for par tomorrow because there is so much experience on the leaderboard. I hope my putter gets going because I think I'll need 65 to win.'

Everyone agreed. Brad Faxon, the co-leader with Zoeller, predicted the winner would have to shoot three or four under par. 'Particularly if it's a day like this,' he said.

Still dreaming of winning his sixth Open Championship, which would equal Harry Vardon's record, Tom Watson said, 'Nature had produced an easy course for us this year. It's going to take something in the middle 60s to win.' Then, showing how he felt about the weather, he grinned and added, 'I hope the wind blows 40 miles an hour tomorrow.'

Of course it didn't. If anything, the weather turned

Two birdies increased Parnevik's lead to three strokes.

Parnevik thought he needed to birdie the 18th, and went for the flag with a wedge. The ball fell short, and he bogeyed.

Fuzzy Zoeller held on to third place with his level-par 70.

milder and a touch warmer. The wind had shifted to the northeast, but it had negligible effect on the shots, and once again the sun sparkled on the sea. It was indeed a rare Scottish summer day, another made for low-scoring golf.

Perhaps the tension associated with the final round had its effect, but the field scored nowhere near as well as it had the previous day. Where 42 men had broken 70 in the third round, only 29 came in under par in the last, raising the total to 148 rounds under 70 for the championship, which was 32 more than the previous record in 1993 at Royal St George's.

Once again, some of those scores were indeed low. Both Faldo and the Swede Anders Forsbrand shot 64s early in the day, which moved them both into the top 10 places. Russell Claydon, the former Walker Cup player, shot 65, both Price and the American Bob Estes shot 66s, Parnevik was among four at 67, while 13 others shot 68 and seven more shot 69.

Naturally, the average score rose as well. It is difficult to grasp that an average of 70.70 for an 81-man field doesn't measure up to standard, but a day earlier these same players had shot an average score of 69.39. Back in the middle 1940s, in his greatest year, Byron Nelson had earned everlasting fame by averaging 68.33 over an entire season. He would have felt at home in this company, which should give some indications of just how well the field had been playing.

When Faldo sped around the first nine in 32, everyone suspected that the championship record of 267, set only a year earlier, must surely be in jeopardy. With 201, Zoeller and Faxon would have to shoot 66 to match it, which wasn't out of the question since both had shot a better score than that already. Price, Parnevik, Watson and Ronan Rafferty would need 65, and both Rafferty and Watson had done it, and Price and Parnevik had missed by one.

Faldo came back in 32 as well and shot 64. It is a measure of the man, though, that he wasn't satisfied. Hopelessly out of the running for the championship, he found some lofty goal to aim for. When he rifled a three iron about 20 feet from the hole on the 17th, he said to himself, 'If I hole this putt and then birdie the 18th, I'll shoot 62, and that's never been done be-

Out of contention, Nick Faldo tied for eighth with his 64.

Anders Forsbrand also shot 64 to tie for fourth place.

fore.' That he didn't doesn't matter.

Faldo had shown it could be done, and two hours later Forsbrand came in with his own 64 to confirm it. The lesson, however, somehow seemed lost on everyone else, for this was a strange sort of day. Throughout the first nine everyone played a reserved sort of golf. The six men who began the day within one stroke of one another made more bogeys than birdies on the first nine, and the championship didn't really come alive until they all turned for home.

There were, however, a couple of interesting moments, the first when Larry Mize holed his pitch on the first hole for an eagle 2 and then birdied the third, which pulled him down to seven under par, within two strokes of the lead. But after going out in 32 and clinging close to the leaders, he lost his momentum on the home nine, came back in 38 and finished in a tie for 11th place.

Watson gave everyone a thrill with a tentative move at the seventh, where he birdied once again and held a share of the lead for one brief moment. It ended quickly and sadly when his game utterly collapsed. Failing to hole the troublesome three- and four-foot putts that have so bedeviled him, Watson made 6s on both the eighth and ninth, a pair of par 4s, and played no further part in the championship except to encourage Parnevik, his pairing mate. Nor could Zoeller or Faxon make something happen.

Russell Claydon slipped into the top 20 with his 65.

David Feherty shot 70 with only one birdie.

Brad Faxon's putting carried him only so far.

Fuzzy compared his round to sitting in a room watching paint dry.

All the excitement of the glorious finish was left to the second nine, when first Parnevik and then Price stormed through the final holes to as gripping a finish as this championship had seen since Watson's duel with Nicklaus here in 1977.

Faxon, a lean redhead, had made a bet with Ben Crenshaw, Corey Pavin and Davis Love during a practice round. If any of them played a bogey-free round, the others would pay him US$1,000 (about £625) each. Faxon won the bet.

The next day as the championship began, he bogeyed three of the first 13 holes, but since then he had played 41 holes without another. Over that span of holes he had shown only one 5 on his scorecard, a par on the seventh in the third round. In those last two rounds, when he had shot 65 and 67, he had clawed his way to a share of the lead and put himself in the running for the game's biggest prize. Before the final round began he told himself he was in the best position he had ever been in, but his private talks had no effect.

Faxon simply had no more to give. After a fine opening drive, he played a pitch to the first that had nothing on it. His ball raced across the green and

into the rough beyond. A timid pitch followed by a missed putt and Faxon had his first bogey in 42 holes. A few more would follow, and while Faxon hung close to the leaders, his finely-tuned putting stroke could carry him no further.

One of the wonders of this championship was that Zoeller hung on for third place, for the putts simply wouldn't fall for him either. More than one singed the edge of the cup but slipped past, and yet he was never far from the lead. As late as the ninth hole, when he missed a shortish putt for a par 4, he shared first place with four others at eight under par; Zoeller, Price and Rafferty had played through the ninth, Parnevik through the 10th, and David Feherty the 11th.

At that stage no one could be quite sure who to follow, for no one was playing first-class golf. How Price managed to hang on baffled everyone, for he seemed to be hitting the ball everywhere.

With none of the others moving ahead, and indeed some dropping further behind, Parnevik began to take over. He had made nothing but pars through the first 10 holes, but here he broke the pattern. Standing on the tee of the 11th, the par 3, he played a solid six iron within 15 feet of the cup and holed it. Now he stood at nine under par and had gone out ahead for the first time. A drive into the 12th fairway, then an eight iron dead on line to the hole pulled up six feet short. Once more the putt fell. He was 10 under par now, ahead by two strokes.

He hit another solid drive on the 13th and a nine iron about four feet from the hole. Again he holed. He was 11 under par. He was playing superb golf, but that last birdie had picked up no ground, for Price had birdied the 12th and Zoeller the 11th with a stunning five iron no more than a foot and a half from the cup. They stood at nine under par, with Feherty at eight under.

After a regulation par 4 at the 14th, Parnevik missed the 15th green and bogeyed. Still ahead, his lead had been cut to a single stroke.

Price, meanwhile, had been living a charmed life. He had gone out in 35, even par, with two birdies written off by two bogeys, pulled his four-iron ap-

Tom Kite tied for eighth with 69.

Colin Montgomerie also shot 69 to tie with Kite and Faldo.

Tom Watson was again short of Harry Vardon's record.

proach to the left of the 10th green, played an indifferent pitch to about 15 feet, then holed the putt for the par. A routine par 3 at the 11th, and then an eight iron to 15 feet on the 12th set up his third birdie of the round.

Once again, though, he found trouble. After missing the 13th green, he played a nerveless pitch that left him a missable four-foot putt, but he stood up to the challenge and ran it home. Then he played a five iron into the 14th that had nothing on it. The ball streaked across the green, through the gallery, and ran at least 25 yards beyond. Speaking of it later, he said he couldn't believe how far it had gone. He seemed certain to bogey, but once again he called on his determination not to give in.

He played a wonderful running seven iron that rolled along the nearly bare ground, hopped on to the green, and pulled up no more than four feet from the cup. He holed the putt and saved not only his round but the championship as well.

It was difficult at the time to estimate the importance of those two saves, but reflecting on them later, Price claimed they were keys to his winning by saying, 'The whole round was set up by 13 and 14.' Then he admitted, 'In previous years I may not have got them up and down. They were equally important as my putts on 16 and 17.'

Still, he lagged behind Parnevik, who was about to make his final run. Ten under par after the 15th, Jesper played a nice pitch into the 16th and holed from about 15 feet to slip to 11 under par once again, and moved on to the 17th, an almost-certain birdie hole. It had already given up 38 birdies and seven eagles that day alone.

Parnevik played a one iron off the tee and a four iron that turned slightly and lighted in the rough left and short of the green. Jesper played a perfectly gauged little pitch-and-run that stopped about four feet right of the hole. The putt fell and as far as almost everyone could tell, he had won the Open.

Now he made an unfortunate mistake.

Although scoreboards were just about everywhere you looked, Parnevik didn't bother to check to be certain of how he stood. He had heard constant cheering behind him, and not realizing some of those

Ronan Rafferty chipped-in at the 12th, but shot 74.

It was 'Well Done Nick' and 'See You At St Andrews' in 1995.

cheers were the result of hard-won pars, he assumed he needed a birdie on the last hole. He didn't.

After a drive to the right edge of the fairway, he decided to go for the flagstick with a pitching wedge. He simply didn't have enough club. The ball fell short against a grassy bank, his recovery fell too far short of the hole, and he bogeyed.

Against this backdrop, Price had holed from 14 feet on the 16th for a birdie, and then made his eagle 3, picking up three strokes on two holes.

'I couldn't believe the putt on 17 went in,' Price said later. 'I knew walking up to that green I had to make that putt. When it jumped in, I just about jumped out of my skin.'

Indeed he did. As it dropped, Nick leaped off the ground and ran around, waving his putter aloft. Now he knew he had the championship provided he made no mistakes on the home hole.

He took no chances. A three iron from the tee and a safe seven iron to the middle of the green left him 25 feet from the cup. He lagged his first putt within two feet, studied it first, then rolled it in.

Clutching the gleaming silver claret jug, Price said, 'In 1982 I had my left hand on the trophy. In 1988 I had my right hand on the trophy. Now, finally, I have both hands on it.'

At the ceremony, Price told Parnevik, 'You have youth on your side. I hope you'll use it wisely.'

One of the most spectacular scenes in sport is the 18th hole of the Open Championship, especially at Turnberry.

FOURTH ROUND RESULTS

HOLE	1	2	3	4	5	6	7	8	9	10	11	12	13	14	15	16	17	18	
PAR	4	4	4	3	4	3	5	4	4	4	3	4	4	4	3	4	5	4	TOTAL
Nick Price	4	5	4	2	5	3	4	4	4	4	3	3	4	4	3	3	3	4	66-268
Jesper Parnevik	4	4	4	3	4	3	5	4	4	4	2	3	3	4	4	3	4	5	67-269
Fuzzy Zoeller	4	3	4	3	4	4	5	4	5	4	2	4	5	4	3	4	5	3	70-271
Anders Forsbrand	4	4	4	2	4	3	5	4	3	3	2	4	4	4	3	4	3	4	64-273
Mark James	4	4	4	2	4	4	5	4	4	4	3	4	4	6	2	4	3	3	68-273
David Feherty	4	4	4	3	4	3	4	4	4	3	3	4	4	4	3	4	6	4	70-273
Brad Faxon	5	4	4	3	4	4	5	4	4	5	3	4	4	4	3	4	5	4	73-274
Nick Faldo	3	4	5	3	4	2	3	4	4	3	3	4	4	4	3	3	4	4	64-275
Tom Kite	3	3	4	2	4	3	5	5	5	5	2	4	4	4	3	3	4	6	69-275
Colin Montgomerie	4	4	4	3	4	3	5	4	4	4	2	5	3	4	3	4	5	4	69-275
Russell Claydon	4	5	3	2	4	4	3	4	4	4	3	3	3	3	4	4	4	4	65-276
Mark McNulty	4	4	4	3	3	2	4	4	5	4	3	4	4	3	4	3	5	68-276
Frank Nobilo	4	5	5	2	4	3	4	4	4	4	3	4	4	2	3	5	4	68-276
Jonathan Lomas	3	4	4	3	4	3	5	4	4	4	2	4	4	4	4	4	4	68-276
Mark Calcavecchia	6	4	4	3	4	3	4	4	5	4	2	4	3	4	3	4	3	4	68-276
Greg Norman	4	3	4	3	4	3	4	4	5	3	3	4	5	4	3	4	5	5	69-276
Larry Mize	2	4	3	3	4	3	5	4	4	4	4	5	5	3	4	5	4	70-276
Tom Watson	4	4	4	3	4	3	4	6	6	4	3	4	4	4	3	4	5	5	74-276
Ronan Rafferty	5	4	4	4	4	3	3	4	4	6	2	3	5	4	3	6	4	6	74-276

HOLE SUMMARY

HOLE	PAR	EAGLES	BIRDIES	PARS	BOGEYS	HIGHER	RANK	AVERAGE
1	4	1	9	56	14	1	12	4.06
2	4	0	9	56	14	2	8	4.12
3	4	0	7	55	19	0	6	4.15
4	3	0	17	57	7	0	16	2.88
5	4	0	7	59	12	3	7	4.14
6	3	0	5	56	19	1	2	3.21
7	5	8	31	39	3	0	17	4.46
8	4	0	5	58	17	1	4	4.17
9	4	0	5	50	24	2	2	4.28
OUT	35	9	95	486	129	10		35.47
10	4	0	13	49	17	2	9	4.10
11	3	0	17	56	7	1	15	2.90
12	4	0	15	48	13	5	9	4.10
13	4	0	8	53	18	2	4	4.17
14	4	0	9	60	11	1	13	4.05
15	3	0	11	57	13	0	14	3.02
16	4	0	12	56	8	5	9	4.10
17	5	8	40	28	5	0	18	4.37
18	4	0	6	39	32	4	1	4.42
IN	35	8	131	446	124	20		35.23
TOTAL	70	17	226	932	253	30		70.70

		LOW SCORES		
Players Below Par	29			
Players At Par	11	Low First Nine	Bob Estes	31
Players Above Par	41	Low Second Nine	Mark Brooks	30
		Low Round	Nick Faldo	64
			Anders Forsbrand	64

CHAMPIONSHIP HOLE SUMMARY

HOLE	PAR	EAGLES	BIRDIES	PARS	BOGEYS	HIGHER	RANK	AVERAGE
1	4	2	60	331	73	8	13	4.05
2	4	0	52	325	92	5	11	4.11
3	4	0	53	285	133	3	8	4.18
4	3	1	102	332	39	0	16	2.86
5	4	0	50	308	100	16	8	4.18
6	3	0	38	294	126	16	1	3.26
7	5	27	186	223	32	6	17	4.59
8	4	0	31	299	127	17	3	4.27
9	4	0	36	326	104	8	8	4.18
OUT	35	30	608	2723	826	79		35.68
10	4	0	63	332	73	6	13	4.05
11	3	0	89	335	46	4	15	2.93
12	4	1	41	259	152	21	2	4.32
13	4	0	49	296	116	13	5	4.20
14	4	1	41	300	119	13	4	4.22
15	3	0	52	308	108	6	5	3.15
16	4	1	78	304	64	27	12	4.09
17	5	26	221	203	23	1	18	4.48
18	4	0	56	286	119	13	7	4.19
IN	35	29	690	2623	820	104		35.63
TOTAL	70	59	1298	5346	1646	183		71.31

	FIRST ROUND	SECOND ROUND	THIRD ROUND	FOURTH ROUND	TOTAL
Players Below Par	30	47	42	29	148
Players At Par	8	15	10	11	44
Players Above Par	118	94	29	41	282

ATTENDANCE

PRACTICE ROUNDS	23,000
FIRST ROUND	25,000
SECOND ROUND	25,000
THIRD ROUND	30,000
FOURTH ROUND	25,000
TOTAL	128,000

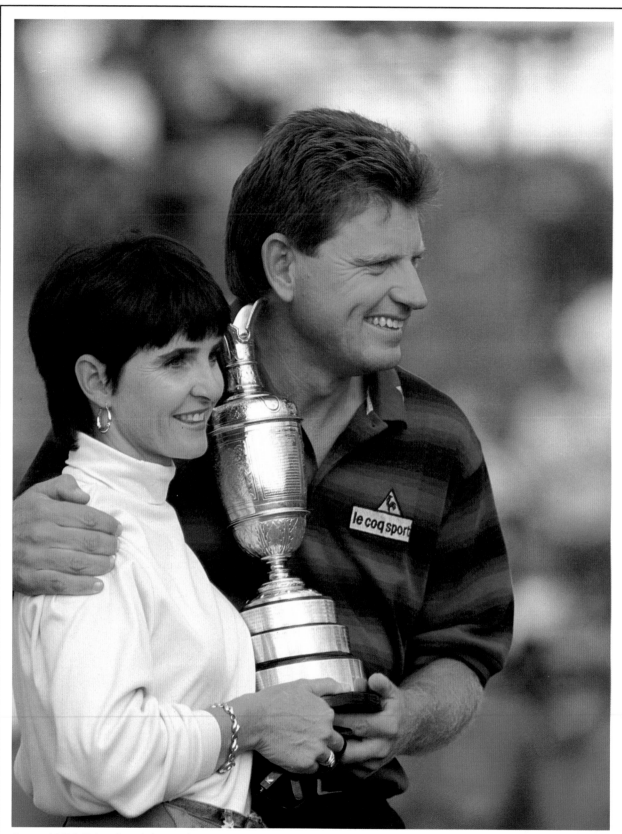

Sue and Nick Price shared the trophy, as they had their years together as Price climbed in international golf.

HE PLAYED LIKE A CHAMPION

BY JOHN HOPKINS

'Nice' is a word that can have many different meanings without really meaning anything. 'Have a nice day,' say the Americans. 'Was the weather nice?' ask the British. 'Did you have a nice time?' So we must not describe Nick Price, the Open champion, as nice, though everyone does because he is. Tall, friendly, gifted, handsome — these and any dozen other adjectives are all acceptable currency. But nice, never. Price can't stand the word. 'I would rather be known as a friendly, approachable person,' he said. 'Nice is such a generic term; I think it's a very poor word in the English dictionary because it encompasses so many things.'

• • •

Two Open Championships that he did not win helped Nicholas Raymond Liege Price win his first. Price, 25, was playing in the fourth round of the 1982 Open at Royal Troon. At the time he was a regular competitor on the PGA European Tour, a decent fellow, a popular chap.

After successive birdies on the 10th, 11th and 12th, Price led by three strokes. Then he let slip the fateful words to his caddie, the ones that brought down such hubris on his shoulders, 'Well, we've got it now.' The moment he said that was the moment he had *not* got it. He unravelled spectacularly, losing one stroke at the 13th and two at the 15th and finishing one stroke behind Tom Watson.

Later that week I tracked Price down. He was in London staying with a friend. On the telephone he was warm, thoughtful and helpful. He sounded as though he had come to terms with what had happened at Troon. He did not sound bitter nor filled with self pity. He was pragmatic. On all our subsequent meetings, Price demonstrated he had quickly acquired the American characteristic of being able to remember the names and faces of the people who

cropped up regularly if infrequently in his life.

'How's it' is invariably his greeting, which sounds like a shortened form of 'How is it going?' mixed in with 'How is it, man?,' the sort of greeting you hear in South Africa.

In the months and years to come, Price would remember what he had learned from the Troon Open, and it would help him. There were moments in the 1980s when he needed as much help as he could get. He was the 'nearly man,' someone who would feature in an event but never win it. His was the back others used to leapfrog over.

In 1986 he set a course record of 63 at Augusta only to be elbowed aside in the pandemonium surrounding Jack Nicklaus' sixth US Masters victory. In 1988 he started the final day of the Open at Royal Lytham with a two-stroke lead, only to be the victim of one of the greatest closing rounds ever, a 65 by Seve Ballesteros. When Price withdrew from the 1991 USPGA to be with his pregnant wife, his place was taken by an unknown player, John Daly, and we all know what happened to him.

'I would get in a position to win,' Price says, 'and something would go wrong every time. It would be a wedge shot, a chip or a putt or I would drive in a bush somewhere. I kept hitting the wrong shots at the wrong time.' After his first victory in America in the 1983 World Series of Golf, he did not win again until 1991. His swing looked good, if a little fast, but it was proving inefficient under the greatest pressure, making him erratic.

'For years, there was nothing between brilliant and awful,' Price said. 'If the timing was there, then it could be 65. If it wasn't, it could be 80. There didn't seem to be anything in between. I played my first years essentially on talent. Anyone with a trained eye looking at my swing now, and imagining it 20 times worse, would see where it was in the mid-80s. There was no consistency to what I was doing. One day I

Price completed nine holes in level par, with two birdies and two bogeys, and needed to do better on the final nine.

would adjust my grip, the next do something else. Finally, I knew if I was to make a living at this game, I would have to make some changes.'

He began to slow his swing down. By 1992, he had done this by as much as 60 percent, by his own estimate. An intelligent man, he started improving the quality of his mind, as well, by doing more reading. *Mental Toughness for Sport* and *The Psychology of Winning* were two books he kept on his bedside table. Between 1984 and 1990, he fluctuated between 22nd and 80th on the American money list.

In 1991, he won twice in the United States, finishing seventh on the money list. He improved on this with a solid and popular success in the 1992 USPGA Championship at Bellerive Country Club in St Louis, and moved to fourth in the money list. The USPGA was a watershed for him. If he could hardly win before then, he could hardly lose after it. In 1993 he captured The Players Championship, won three tour-

naments in consecutive starts, set a PGA Tour record for money winnings of nearly $1.5 million and was voted Player of the Year. No one was saying he was a 'nearly man' now.

The change was as a result of getting married and finding the maturity, perspective and peace of mind that often comes with marriage. At the same time, the alterations he had been making to his swing under the direction of David Leadbetter began to bear fruit.

Leadbetter and Faldo are a well-known pair; Leadbetter and Price, who grew up at the same time in Zimbabwe, are less so. Here is Price on Leadbetter: 'He is a very introverted person, which may be to his detriment. But if you disagree with something he says, he encourages you to bring it up, to give him your opinion. He listens to you and tries to understand what you are saying. I must say that of all the times I have disagreed with him, he has always shown me where I was wrong. He says "I understand your point but consider this ..." and then he guides you into an understanding of what he is talking about.'

Here is Leadbetter on Price and Faldo: 'Every player is different, and as a coach you have to respect that. Faldo is more mechanical whereas Nicky is more of a sprinter, I suppose. He'll say "come and watch for five or 10 minutes" and "How's this looking, OK?" and "I've got it, thanks." Faldo could spend 365 days a year working on it, and it wouldn't bother him.'

In previewing of the 123rd Open Championship, I wrote in *The Times*: 'Price is the most consistent and successful player in the world, competing in more events than either Faldo or Norman. Victory in the recent Western Open was his third of the year. However, doubts remain about the Zimbabwean's performance in major championships, which are not as good as they should be. He has missed the cut in two of the past six championships and has come 31st and 35th in two others. If he is to establish himself as the outstanding player that everyone says he is, he needs more than one major championship to his name. Turnberry would be a good place to start.'

He took me at my word. He arrived in Scotland having won three events in the United States, including the last event he had entered. In a quiet moment before the start, he admitted he was better prepared than for any recent major championship, and as a consequence he felt more confident. He had brought only a couple of putters with him to Scotland, whereas he had taken five to Oakmont for the US Open one month earlier. In short, he seemed to be saying he was as ready as he could be.

Then at Turnberry he concluded his championship like the lion-hearted competitor he had not been 12 years earlier but had become in the interim. Birdie, eagle and par over the 70th, 71st and 72nd holes gave him a 66 that included two three-putts in the first five holes. Nobody could quibble about that sort of scoring. It is no good belittling Price's effort by saying that Jesper Parnevik threw it away.

Price won his second major championship in a way that separates great champions from lesser champions, and run-of-the-mill champions from ordinary

An eight iron to 15 feet at the 12th set up Price's third birdie.

Price saved par — and possibly the championship — with a running shot at the 14th that stopped four feet from the hole.

competitors. He knew the size of the task in hand and, summoning every ounce of concentration and energy, he achieved it.

Judged by the highest standards, one conclusion is that Parnevik has only himself to blame, just as Price had only himself to blame at Troon in 1982. Parnevik stood on the 18th tee, the 72nd hole, with a three-stroke lead. Moments later, Price holed for a birdie on the 16th. Then Parnevik gambled with his second shot to the 18th, a gamble that failed when his ball ended short and slightly left of the green with a nasty step between him and the flag. A bogey 5 was inevitable. This was followed by Price holing that enormous putt for an eagle on the 17th, the stroke that gave him the cushion — and ultimate margin of victory — of one stroke.

Sport provides an acceptable litmus test of a person's resolve. Prove that you have it at one shining moment and you will probably win, as Price did on this occasion; if you do not, you will probably lose as Parnevik did. Parnevik demonstrated himself unprepared to become champion on the 18th tee. He had refused to look at the leaderboards on the way round and believed he needed a birdie to win. Not only that, his caddie did not tell him any different.

It is inconceivable in a similar situation that Tom Watson, Jack Nicklaus, Seve Ballesteros, Nick Faldo or Price would have begun to select a club, never mind played a stroke, without knowing precisely the disposition of their rivals. If Parnevik thought that by ignoring the state of play of those around him he would lighten the crushing load of pressure on his shoulders, he was not worthy of being in that position at that time. True champions are those who survive the pressure when it is at its greatest. They do not try and hide from it.

Now that Price has proved himself a worthy champion we should say 'Thank you and well done.' We should not, as Americans might, say 'Nice job, Nick.' And please, no more 'Price Is Right' headlines. Let us give him credit for being a good bloke, the sort of man you want to be partnered with in a pro-am, and a man who played like a champion to win the Open. Remember, he can't stand the word 'nice.'

With a birdie, eagle, par finish, Price was Open champion after his disappointments of 1982 and 1988.

Gary Player (1959, 1968, 1974) was celebrating 40 years of competition in the Open Championship.

RECORDS OF THE OPEN CHAMPIONSHIP

MOST VICTORIES
6, Harry Vardon, 1896-98-99-1903-11-14
5, James Braid, 1901-05-06-08-10; J.H. Taylor, 1894-95-1900-09-13; Peter Thomson, 1954-55-56-58-65; Tom Watson, 1975-77-80-82-83

MOST TIMES RUNNER-UP OR JOINT RUNNER-UP
7, Jack Nicklaus, 1964-67-68-72-76-77-79
6, J.H. Taylor, 1896-1904-05-06-07-14

OLDEST WINNER
Old Tom Morris, 46 years 99 days, 1867
Roberto de Vicenzo, 44 years 93 days, 1967

YOUNGEST WINNER
Young Tom Morris, 17 years 5 months 8 days, 1868
Willie Auchterlonie, 21 years 24 days, 1893
Severiano Ballesteros, 22 years 3 months 12 days, 1979

YOUNGEST AND OLDEST COMPETITOR
John Ball, 14 years, 1878
Gene Sarazen, 71 years 4 months 13 days, 1973

BIGGEST MARGIN OF VICTORY
13 strokes, Old Tom Morris, 1862
12 strokes, Young Tom Morris, 1870
8 strokes, J.H. Taylor, 1900 and 1913; James Braid, 1908
6 strokes, Bobby Jones, 1927; Walter Hagen, 1929; Arnold Palmer, 1962; Johnny Miller, 1976

LOWEST WINNING AGGREGATES
267 (66, 68, 69, 64), Greg Norman, Royal St George's, 1993
268 (68, 70, 65, 65), Tom Watson, Turnberry, 1977; (69, 66, 67, 66), Nick Price, Turnberry, 1994
270 (67, 65, 67, 71), Nick Faldo, St Andrews, 1990
271 (68, 70, 64, 69), Tom Watson, Muirfield, 1980

LOWEST AGGREGATES BY RUNNER-UP
269 (68, 70, 65, 66), Jack Nicklaus, Turnberry, 1977; (69, 63, 70, 67), Nick Faldo, Royal St George's, 1993; (68, 66, 68, 67), Jesper Parnevik, Turnberry, 1994
273 (66, 67, 70, 70), John Cook, Muirfield, 1992

LOWEST AGGREGATE BY AN AMATEUR
281 (68, 72, 70, 71), Iain Pyman, Royal St George's, 1993

LOWEST INDIVIDUAL ROUND
63, Mark Hayes, second round, Turnberry, 1977; Isao Aoki, third round, Muirfield, 1980; Greg Norman, second round, Turnberry, 1986; Paul Broadhurst, third round, St Andrews, 1990; Jodie Mudd, fourth round, Royal Birkdale, 1991; Nick Faldo, second round, and Payne Stewart, fourth round, Royal St George's, 1993

LOWEST INDIVIDUAL ROUND BY AN AMATEUR
66, Frank Stranahan, fourth round, Troon, 1950

LOWEST FIRST ROUND
64, Craig Stadler, Royal Birkdale, 1983; Christy O'Connor Jr., Royal St George's, 1985; Rodger Davis, Muirfield, 1987; Raymond Floyd and Steve Pate, Muirfield, 1992

LOWEST SECOND ROUND
63, Mark Hayes, Turnberry, 1977; Greg Norman, Turnberry, 1986; Nick Faldo, Royal St George's, 1993

LOWEST THIRD ROUND
63, Isao Aoki, Muirfield, 1980; Paul Broadhurst, St Andrews, 1990

LOWEST FOURTH ROUND
63, Jodie Mudd, Royal Birkdale, 1991; Payne Stewart, Royal St George's, 1993

LOWEST FIRST 36 HOLES
130 (66, 64), Nick Faldo, Muirfield, 1992
132 (67, 65), Henry Cotton, Sandwich, 1934; (66, 66), Greg Norman and (67, 65), Nick Faldo, St Andrews, 1990; (69, 63), Nick Faldo, Royal St George's, 1993

LOWEST SECOND 36 HOLES
130 (65, 65), Tom Watson, Turnberry, 1977; (64, 66), Ian Baker-Finch, Royal Birkdale, 1991

LOWEST FIRST 54 HOLES
199 (67, 65, 67), Nick Faldo, St Andrews, 1990; (66, 64, 69), Nick Faldo, Muirfield, 1992

LOWEST FINAL 54 HOLES
199 (66, 67, 66), Nick Price, Turnberry, 1994
200 (70, 65, 65), Tom Watson, Turnberry, 1977; (63, 70, 67), Nick Faldo, Royal St George's, 1993; (66, 64, 70), Fuzzy Zoeller, Turnberry, 1994

LOWEST 9 HOLES
28, Denis Durnian, first 9, Royal Birkdale, 1983
29, Peter Thomson and Tom Haliburton, first 9, Royal Lytham, 1958; Tony Jacklin, first 9, St Andrews, 1970; Bill Longmuir, first 9, Royal Lytham, 1979; David J. Russell, first 9, Royal Lytham, 1988; Ian Baker-Finch and Paul Broadhurst, first 9, St Andrews, 1990; Ian Baker-Finch, first 9, Royal Birkdale, 1991

CHAMPIONS IN THREE DECADES
Harry Vardon, 1896, 1903, 1911
J.H. Taylor, 1894, 1900, 1913
Gary Player, 1959, 1968, 1974

BIGGEST SPAN BETWEEN FIRST AND LAST VICTORIES
19 years, J.H. Taylor, 1894-1913
18 years, Harry Vardon, 1896-1914
15 years, Gary Player, 1959-74
14 years, Henry Cotton, 1934-48

SUCCESSIVE VICTORIES
4, Young Tom Morris, 1868-72. No championship in 1871
3, Jamie Anderson, 1877-79; Bob Ferguson, 1880-82, Peter Thomson, 1954-56
2, Old Tom Morris, 1861-62; J.H. Taylor, 1894-95; Harry Vardon, 1898-99; James Braid, 1905-06; Bobby Jones, 1926-27; Walter Hagen, 1928-29; Bobby Locke, 1949-50; Arnold Palmer, 1961-62; Lee Trevino, 1971-72; Tom Watson, 1982-83

VICTORIES BY AMATEURS
3, Bobby Jones, 1926-27-30
2, Harold Hilton, 1892-97
1, John Ball, 1890
Roger Wethered lost a play-off in 1921

HIGHEST NUMBER OF TOP FIVE FINISHES
16, J.H. Taylor, Jack Nicklaus
15, Harry Vardon, James Braid

HIGHEST NUMBER OF ROUNDS UNDER 70
31, Jack Nicklaus
29, Nick Faldo
26, Tom Watson
21, Lee Trevino
20, Greg Norman
19, Severiano Ballesteros
18, Nick Price
16, Bernhard Langer
15, Peter Thomson, Gary Player
13, Ben Crenshaw, Raymond Floyd, Tom Kite

OUTRIGHT LEADER AFTER EVERY ROUND
Willie Auchterlonie, 1893; J.H. Taylor, 1894 and 1900; James Braid, 1908; Ted Ray, 1912; Bobby Jones, 1927; Gene Sarazen, 1932; Henry Cotton, 1934; Tom Weiskopf, 1973

RECORD LEADS (SINCE 1892)
After 18 holes:
4 strokes, James Braid, 1908; Bobby Jones, 1927; Henry Cotton, 1934; Christy O'Connor Jr., 1985

After 36 holes:
9 strokes, Henry Cotton, 1934
After 54 holes:
10 strokes, Henry Cotton, 1934
7 strokes, Tony Lema, 1964
6 strokes, James Braid, 1908
5 strokes, Arnold Palmer, 1962; Bill Rogers, 1981; Nick Faldo, 1990

CHAMPIONS WITH EACH ROUND LOWER THAN PREVIOUS ONE
Jack White, 1904, Sandwich, (80, 75, 72, 69)
James Braid, 1906, Muirfield, (77, 76, 74, 73)
Ben Hogan, 1953, Carnoustie, (73, 71, 70, 68)
Gary Player, 1959, Muirfield, (75, 71, 70, 68)

CHAMPION WITH FOUR ROUNDS THE SAME
Densmore Shute, 1933, St Andrews, (73, 73, 73, 73) (excluding the play-off)

BIGGEST VARIATION BETWEEN ROUNDS OF A CHAMPION
14 strokes, Henry Cotton, 1934, second round 65, fourth round 79
11 strokes, Jack White, 1904, first round 80, fourth round 69; Greg Norman, 1986, first round 74, second round 63, third round 74

BIGGEST VARIATION BETWEEN TWO ROUNDS
17 strokes, Jack Nicklaus, 1981, first round 83, second round 66; Ian Baker-Finch, 1986, first round 86, second round 69

BEST COMEBACK BY CHAMPIONS
After 18 holes:
Harry Vardon, 1896, 11 strokes behind the leader
After 36 holes:
George Duncan, 1920, 13 strokes behind the leader
After 54 holes:
Jim Barnes, 1925, 5 strokes behind the leader
Of non-champions, Greg Norman, 1989, 7 strokes behind the leader and lost in a play-off

CHAMPIONS WITH FOUR ROUNDS UNDER 70
Greg Norman, 1993, Royal St George's, (66, 68, 69, 64); Nick Price, 1994, Turnberry, (69, 66, 67, 66)
Of non-champions:
Ernie Els, 1993, Royal St George's, (68, 69, 69, 68); Jesper Parnevik, 1994, Turnberry, (68, 66, 68, 67)

BEST FINISHING ROUND BY A CHAMPION
64, Greg Norman, Royal St George's, 1993
65, Tom Watson, Turnberry, 1977; Severiano Ballesteros, Royal Lytham, 1988
66, Johnny Miller, Royal Birkdale, 1976; Ian Baker-Finch, Royal Birkdale, 1991; Nick Price, Turnberry, 1994

WORST FINISHING ROUND BY A CHAMPION SINCE 1920
79, Henry Cotton, Sandwich, 1934
78, Reg Whitcombe, Sandwich, 1938
77, Walter Hagen, Hoylake, 1924

WORST OPENING ROUND BY A CHAMPION SINCE 1919

80, George Duncan, Deal, 1920 (he also had a second round of 80)
77, Walter Hagen, Hoylake, 1924

BEST OPENING ROUND BY A CHAMPION

66, Peter Thomson, Royal Lytham, 1958; Nick Faldo, Muirfield, 1992; Greg Norman, Royal St George's, 1993
67, Henry Cotton, Sandwich, 1934; Tom Watson, Royal Birkdale, 1983; Severiano Ballesteros, Royal Lytham, 1988; Nick Faldo, St Andrews, 1990

BIGGEST RECOVERY IN 18 HOLES BY A CHAMPION

George Duncan, Deal, 1920, was 13 strokes behind the leader, Abe Mitchell, after 36 holes and level after 54

MOST APPEARANCES ON FINAL DAY (SINCE 1892)

30, J.H. Taylor
29, Jack Nicklaus
27, Harry Vardon, James Braid
26, Peter Thomson
25, Gary Player
23, Dai Rees
22, Henry Cotton

CHAMPIONSHIP WITH HIGHEST NUMBER OF ROUNDS UNDER 70

148, Turnberry, 1994

CHAMPIONSHIP SINCE 1946 WITH THE FEWEST ROUNDS UNDER 70

St Andrews, 1946; Hoylake, 1947; Portrush, 1951; Hoylake, 1956; Carnoustie, 1968. All had only two rounds under 70

LONGEST COURSE

Carnoustie, 1968, 7252 yd (6631 m)

COURSES MOST OFTEN USED

St Andrews and Prestwick, 24; Muirfield, 14; Sandwich, 12; Hoylake, 10; Royal Lytham, 8; Royal Birkdale, 7; Musselburgh, and Royal Troon, 6; Carnoustie, 5; Turnberry, 3; Deal, 2; Royal Portrush and Prince's, 1

PRIZE MONEY

Year	Total	First Prize
1860	nil	nil
1863	10	nil
1864	16	6
1876	20	20
1889	22	8
1891	28.50	10
1892	110	(Amateur winner)
1893	100	30
1910	125	50
1920	225	75
1927	275	100
1930	400	100
1931	500	100
1946	1,000	150
1949	1,700	300
1953	2,450	500
1954	3,500	750
1955	3,750	1,000
1958	4,850	1,000
1959	5,000	1,000
1960	7,000	1,250
1961	8,500	1,400
1963	8,500	1,500
1965	10,000	1,750
1966	15,000	2,100
1968	20,000	3,000
1969	30,000	4,250
1970	40,000	5,250
1971	45,000	5,500
1972	50,000	5,500
1975	75,000	7,500
1977	100,000	10,000
1978	125,000	12,500
1979	155,000	15,500
1980	200,000	25,000
1982	250,000	32,000
1983	300,000	40,000
1984	451,000	55,000
1985	530,000	65,000
1986	600,000	70,000
1987	650,000	75,000
1988	700,000	80,000
1989	750,000	80,000
1990	825,000	85,000
1991	900,000	90,000
1992	950,000	95,000
1993	1,000,000	100,000
1994	1,100,000	110,000

ATTENDANCE

Year	Attendance
1962	37,098
1963	24,585
1964	35,954
1965	32,927
1966	40,182
1967	29,880
1968	51,819
1969	46,001
1970	81,593
1971	70,076
1972	84,746
1973	78,810
1974	92,796
1975	85,258
1976	92,021
1977	87,615
1978	125,271
1979	134,501
1980	131,610
1981	111,987
1982	133,299
1983	142,892
1984	193,126
1985	141,619
1986	134,261
1987	139,189
1988	191,334
1989	160,639
1990	208,680
1991	189,435
1992	146,427
1993	141,000
1994	128,000

Nick Faldo (1987, 1990, 1992)

Seve Ballesteros (1979, 1984, 1988)

Jack Nicklaus (1966, 1970, 1978) and
six times runner-up.

Tom Watson (1975, 1977, 1980,
1982, 1983)

Mark Calcavecchia (1989)

Greg Norman (1986, 1993)   Ian Baker-Finch (1991)   Bob Charles (1963)

Sandy Lyle (1985)   Lee Trevino (1971, 1972)

PAST RESULTS

* Denotes amateurs

1860 PRESTWICK

Willie Park, Musselburgh	55	59	60	174
Tom Morris Sr, Prestwick	58	59	59	176
Andrew Strath, St Andrews				180
Robert Andrew, Perth				191
George Brown, Blackheath				192

1861 PRESTWICK

Tom Morris Sr, Prestwick	54	56	53	163
Willie Park, Musselburgh	54	54	59	167
William Dow, Musselburgh	59	58	54	171
David Park, Musselburgh	58	57	57	172
Robert Andrew, Perth	58	61	56	175

1862 PRESTWICK

Tom Morris Sr, Prestwick	52	55	56	163
Willie Park, Musselburgh	59	59	58	176
Charles Hunter, Prestwick	60	60	58	178
William Dow, Musselburgh	60	58	63	181
* James Knight, Prestwick	62	61	63	186

1863 PRESTWICK

Willie Park, Musselburgh	56	54	58	168
Tom Morris Sr, Prestwick	56	58	56	170
David Park, Musselburgh	55	63	54	172
Andrew Strath, St Andrews	61	55	58	174
George Brown, St Andrews	58	61	57	176

1864 PRESTWICK

Tom Morris Sr, Prestwick	54	58	55	167
Andrew Strath, St Andrews	56	57	56	169
Robert Andrew, Perth	57	58	60	175
Willie Park, Musselburgh	55	67	55	177
William Dow, Musselburgh	56	58	67	181

1865 Prestwick

Andrew Strath, St Andrews	55	54	53	162
Willie Park, Musselburgh	56	52	56	164
William Dow, Musselburgh				171
Robert Kirk, St Andrews	64	54	55	173
Tom Morris Sr, St Andrews	57	61	56	174

1866 PRESTWICK

Willie Park, Musselburgh	54	56	59	169
David Park, Musselburgh	58	57	56	171
Robert Andrew, Perth	58	59	59	176
Tom Morris Sr, St Andrews	61	58	59	178
Robert Kirk, St Andrews	60	62	58	180

1867 PRESTWICK

Tom Morris Sr, St Andrews	58	54	58	170
Willie Park, Musselburgh	58	56	58	172
Andrew Strath, St Andrews	61	57	56	174
Tom Morris Jr, St Andrews	58	59	58	175
Robert Kirk, St Andrews	57	60	60	177

1868 PRESTWICK

Tom Morris Jr, St Andrews	50	55	52	157
Robert Andrew, Perth	53	54	52	159
Willie Park, Musselburgh	58	50	54	162
Robert Kirk, St Andrews	56	59	56	171
John Allen, Westward Ho!	54	52	63	172
Tom Morris Sr, St Andrews	56	62	58	176

1869 PRESTWICK

Tom Morris Jr, St Andrews	51	54	49	154
Tom Morris Sr, St Andrews	54	50	53	157
* S. Mure Fergusson, Royal and Ancient	57	54	54	165
Robert Kirk, St Andrews	53	58	57	168
David Strath, St Andrews	53	56	60	169
Jamie Anderson, St Andrews	60	56	57	173

1870 PRESTWICK

Tom Morris Jr, St Andrews	47	51	51	149
Bob Kirk, Royal Blackheath	52	52	57	161
David Strath, St Andrews	54	49	58	161
Tom Morris Sr, St Andrews	56	52	54	162
* William Doleman, Musselburgh	57	56	58	171
Willie Park, Musselburgh	60	55	58	173

1871 NO COMPETITION

1872 PRESTWICK

Tom Morris Jr, St Andrews	57	56	53	166
David Strath, St Andrews	56	52	61	169
* William Doleman, Musselburgh	63	60	54	177
Tom Morris Sr, St Andrews	62	60	57	179
David Park, Musselburgh	61	57	61	179

1873 ST ANDREWS

Tom Kidd, St Andrews		91	88	179
Jamie Anderson, St Andrews		91	89	180
Tom Morris Jr, St Andrews		94	89	183
Bob Kirk, Royal Blackheath		91	92	183
David Strath, St Andrews		97	90	187

1874 MUSSELBURGH

Mungo Park, Musselburgh		75	84	159
Tom Morris Jr, St Andrews		83	78	161
George Paxton, Musselburgh		80	82	162
Bob Martin, St Andrews		85	79	164
Jamie Anderson, St Andrews		82	83	165

1875 PRESTWICK

Willie Park, Musselburgh	56	59	51	166
Bob Martin, St Andrews	56	58	54	168
Mungo Park, Musselburgh	59	57	55	171
Robert Ferguson, Musselburgh	58	56	58	172
James Rennie, St Andrews	61	59	57	177

1876 ST ANDREWS

Bob Martin, St Andrews				86 90	176
David Strath, North Berwick				86 90	176
(Martin was awarded the title when Strath refused to play-off)					
Willie Park, Musselburgh				94 89	183
Tom Morris Sr, St Andrews				90 95	185
W. Thomson, Elie				90 95	185
Mungo Park, Musselburgh				95 90	185

1877 MUSSELBURGH

Jamie Anderson, St Andrews	40	42	37	41	160
Bob Pringle, Musselburgh	44	38	40	40	162
Bob Ferguson, Musselburgh	40	40	40	44	164
William Cosgrove, Musselburgh	41	39	44	40	164
David Strath, North Berwick	45	40	38	43	166
William Brown, Musselburgh	39	41	45	41	166

1878 PRESTWICK

Jamie Anderson, St Andrews	53	53	51	157
Bob Kirk, St Andrews	53	55	51	159
J.O.F. Morris, St Andrews	50	56	55	161
Bob Martin, St Andrews	57	53	55	165
* John Ball, Hoylake	53	57	55	165
Willie Park, Musselburgh	53	56	57	166
William Cosgrove, Musselburgh	53	56	55	166

1879 ST ANDREWS

Jamie Anderson, St Andrews		84 85	169
James Allan, Westward Ho!		88 84	172
Andrew Kirkaldy, St Andrews		86 86	172
George Paxton, Musselburgh			174
Tom Kidd, St Andrews			175
Bob Ferguson, Musselburgh			176

1880 MUSSELBURGH

Bob Ferguson, Musselburgh		81 81	162
Peter Paxton, Musselburgh		81 86	167
Ned Cosgrove, Musselburgh		82 86	168
George Paxton, Musselburgh		85 84	169
Bob Pringle, Musselburgh		90 79	169
David Brown, Musselburgh		86 83	169

1881 PRESTWICK

Bob Ferguson, Musselburgh	53	60	57	170
Jamie Anderson, St Andrews	57	60	56	173
Ned Cosgrove, Musselburgh	61	59	57	177
Bob Martin, St Andrews	57	62	59	178
Tom Morris Sr, St Andrews	58	65	58	181
Willie Campbell, Musselburgh	60	56	65	181
Willie Park Jr, Musselburgh	66	57	58	181

1882 ST ANDREWS

Bob Ferguson, Musselburgh		83 88	171
Willie Fernie, Dumfries		88 86	174
Jamie Anderson, St Andrews		87 88	175
John Kirkaldy, St Andrews		86 89	175
Bob Martin, St Andrews		89 86	175
* Fitz Boothby, St Andrews		86 89	175

1883 MUSSELBURGH

Willie Fernie, Dumfries		75 84	159
Bob Ferguson, Musselburgh		78 80	159
(Fernie won play-off 158 to 159)			
Willie Brown, Musselburgh		83 77	160
Bob Pringle, Musselburgh		79 82	161
Willie Campbell, Musselburgh		80 83	163
George Paxton, Musselburgh		80 83	163

1884 PRESTWICK

Jack Simpson, Carnoustie		78 82	160
David Rollan, Elie		81 83	164
Willie Fernie, Felixstowe		80 84	164
Willie Campbell, Musselburgh		84 85	169
Willie Park Jr, Musselburgh		86 83	169

1885 ST ANDREWS

Bob Martin, St Andrews		84 87	171
Archie Simpson, Carnoustie		83 89	172
David Ayton, St Andrews		89 84	173
Willie Fernie, Felixstowe		89 85	174
Willie Park Jr, Musselburgh		86 88	174
Bob Simpson, Carnoustie		85 89	174

1886 MUSSELBURGH

David Brown, Musselburgh		79 78	157
Willie Campbell, Musselburgh		78 81	159
Ben Campbell, Musselburgh		79 81	160
Archie Simpson, Carnoustie		82 79	161
Willie Park Jr, Musselburgh		84 77	161
Thomas Gossett, Musselburgh		82 79	161
Bob Ferguson, Musselburgh		82 79	161

1887 PRESTWICK

Willie Park Jr, Musselburgh		82 79	161
Bob Martin, St Andrews		81 81	162
Willie Campbell, Prestwick		77 87	164
* Johnny Laidlay, Honourable Company		86 80	166
Ben Sayers, North Berwick		83 85	168
Archie Simpson, Carnoustie		81 87	168

1888 ST ANDREWS

Jack Burns, Warwick		86 85	171
David Anderson Jr, St Andrews		86 86	172
Ben Sayers, North Berwick		85 87	172
Willie Campbell, Prestwick		84 90	174
* Leslie Balfour, Edinburgh		86 89	175

1889 MUSSELBURGH

Willie Park Jr, Musselburgh	39	39	39	38	155
Andrew Kirkaldy, St Andrews	39	38	39	39	155
(Park won play-off 158 to 163)					
Ben Sayes, North Berwick	39	40	41	39	159
* Johnny Laidlay, Honourable Company	42	39	40	41	162
David Brown, Musselburgh	43	39	41	39	162

1890 PRESTWICK

* John Ball, Royal Liverpool	82	82		164
Willie Fernie, Troon	85	82		167
Archie Simpson, Carnoustie	85	82		167
Willie Park Jr, Musselburgh	90	80		170
Andrew Kirkaldy, St Andrews	81	89		170

1891 ST ANDREWS

Hugh Kirkaldy, St Andrews	83	83		166
Willie Fernie, Troon	84	84		168
Andrew Kirkaldy, St Andrews	84	84		168
S. Mure Fergusson, Royal and Ancient	86	84		170
W.D. More, Chester	84	87		171
Willie Park Jr, Musselburgh	88	85		173

(From 1892 the competition was extended to 72 holes)

1892 MUIRFIELD

* Harold Hilton, Royal Liverpool	78	81	72	74	305
* John Ball Jr, Royal Liverpool	75	80	74	79	308
James Kirkaldy, St Andrews	77	83	73	75	308
Sandy Herd, Huddersfield	77	78	77	76	308
J. Kay, Seaton Carew	82	78	74	78	312
Ben Sayers, North Berwick	80	76	81	75	312

1893 PRESTWICK

Willie Auchterlonie, St Andrews	78	81	81	82	322
* Johnny Laidlay, Honourable Company	80	83	80	81	324
Sandy Herd, Huddersfield	82	81	78	84	325
Hugh Kirkaldy, St Andrews	83	79	82	82	326
Andrew Kirkaldy, St Andrews	85	82	82	77	326

1894 SANDWICH

J.H. Taylor, Winchester	84	80	81	81	326
Douglas Rolland, Limpsfield	86	79	84	82	331
Andrew Kirkaldy, St Andrews	86	79	83	84	332
A. Toogood, Eltham	84	85	82	82	333
Willie Fernie, Troon	84	84	86	80	334
Harry Vardon, Bury St Edmunds	86	86	82	80	334
Ben Sayers, North Berwick	85	81	84	84	334

1895 ST ANDREWS

J.H. Taylor, Winchester	86	78	80	78	322
Sandy Herd, Huddersfield	82	77	82	85	326
Andrew Kirkaldy, St Andrews	81	83	84	84	332
G. Pulford, Hoylake	84	81	83	87	335
Archie Simpson, Aberdeen	88	85	78	85	336

1896 MUIRFIELD

Harry Vardon, Ganton	83	78	78	77	316
J.H. Taylor, Winchester	77	78	81	80	316
(Vardon won play-off 157 to 161)					
* Freddie G. Tait, Black Watch	83	75	84	77	319
Willie Fernie, Troon	78	79	82	80	319
Sandy Herd, Huddersfield	72	84	79	85	320
James Braid, Romford	83	81	79	80	323

1897 HOYLAKE

* Harold H. Hilton, Royal Liverpool	80	75	84	75	314
James Braid, Romford	80	74	82	79	315
* Freddie G. Tait, Black Watch	79	79	80	79	317
G. Pulford, Hoylake	80	79	79	79	317
Sandy Herd, Huddersfield	78	81	79	80	318
Harry Vardon, Ganton	84	80	80	76	320

1898 PRESTWICK

Harry Vardon, Ganton	79	75	77	76	307
Willie Park, Musselburgh	76	75	78	79	308
* Harold H. Hilton, Royal Liverpool	76	81	77	75	309
J.H. Taylor, Winchester	78	78	77	79	312
* Freddie G. Tait, Black Watch	81	77	75	82	315

1899 SANDWICH

Harry Vardon, Ganton	76	76	81	77	310
Jack White, Seaford	79	79	82	75	315
Andrew Kirkaldy, St Andrews	81	79	82	77	319
J.H. Taylor, Mid-Surrey	77	76	83	84	320
James Braid, Romford	78	78	83	84	322
Willie Fernie, Troon	79	83	82	78	322

1900 ST ANDREWS

J.H. Taylor, Mid-Surrey	79	77	78	75	309
Harry Vardon, Ganton	79	81	80	78	317
James Braid, Romford	82	81	80	79	322
Jack White, Seaford	80	81	82	80	323
Willie Auchterlonie, St Andrews	81	85	80	80	326
Willie Park Jr, Musselburgh	80	83	81	84	328

1901 MUIRFIELD

James Braid, Romford	79	76	74	80	309
Harry Vardon, Ganton	77	78	79	78	312
J.H. Taylor, Mid-Surrey	79	83	74	77	313
* Harold H. Hilton, Royal Liverpool	89	80	75	76	320
Sandy Herd, Huddersfield	87	81	81	76	325
Jack White, Seaford	82	82	80	82	326

1902 HOYLAKE

Sandy Herd, Huddersfield	77	76	73	81	307
Harry Vardon, South Herts	72	77	80	79	308
James Braid, Walton Heath	78	76	80	74	308
R. Maxwell, Honourable Company	79	77	79	74	309
Tom Vardon, Ilkley	80	76	78	79	313
J.H. Taylor, Mid-Surrey	81	76	77	80	314
D. Kinnell, Leven	78	80	79	77	314
* Harold H. Hilton, Royal Liverpool	79	76	81	78	314

1903 PRESTWICK

Harry Vardon, South Herts	73	77	72	78	300
Tom Vardon, Ilkley	76	81	75	74	306
Jack White, Sunningdale	77	78	74	79	308
Sandy Herd, Huddersfield	73	83	76	77	309
James Braid, Walton Heath	77	79	79	75	310

1904 SANDWICH

Jack White, Sunningdale	80	75	72	69	296
James Braid, Walton Heath	77	80	69	71	297
J.H. Taylor, Mid-Surrey	77	78	74	68	297
Tom Vardon, Ilkley	77	77	75	72	301
Harry Vardon, South Herts	76	73	79	74	302

1905 ST ANDREWS

James Braid, Walton Heath	81	78	78	81	318
J.H. Taylor, Mid-Surrey	80	85	78	80	323
R. Jones, Wimbledon Park	81	77	87	78	323
J. Kinnell, Purley Downs	82	79	82	81	324
Arnaud Massy, La Boulie	81	80	82	82	325
E. Gray, Littlehampton	82	81	84	78	325

1906 MUIRFIELD

James Braid, Walton Heath	77	76	74	73	300
J.H. Taylor, Mid-Surrey	77	72	75	80	304
Harry Vardon, South Herts	77	73	77	78	305
* J. Graham Jr, Royal Liverpool	71	79	78	78	306
R. Jones, Wimbledon Park	74	78	73	83	308
Arnaud Massy, La Boulie	76	80	76	78	310

1907 HOYLAKE

Arnaud Massy, La Boulie	76	81	78	77	312
J.H. Taylor, Mid-Surrey	79	79	76	80	314
Tom Vardon, Sandwich	81	81	80	75	317
G. Pulford, Hoylake	81	78	80	78	317
Ted Ray, Ganton	83	80	79	76	318
James Braid, Walton Heath	82	85	75	76	318

1908 PRESTWICK

James Braid, Walton Heath	70	72	77	72	291
Tom Ball, West Lancashire	76	73	76	74	299
Ted Ray, Ganton	79	71	75	76	301
Sandy Herd, Huddersfield	74	74	79	75	302
Harry Vardon, South Herts	79	78	74	75	306
D. Kinnell, Prestwick St Nicholas	75	73	80	78	306

1909 DEAL

J.H. Taylor, Mid-Surrey	74	73	74	74	295
James Braid, Walton Heath	79	73	73	74	299
Tom Ball, West Lancashire	74	75	76	76	301
C. Johns, Southdown	72	76	79	75	302
T.G. Renouf, Manchester	76	78	76	73	303
Ted Ray, Ganton	77	76	76	75	304

1910 ST ANDREWS

James Braid, Walton Heath	76	73	74	76	299
Sandy Herd, Huddersfield	78	74	75	76	303
George Duncan, Hanger Hill	73	77	71	83	304
Laurie Ayton, Bishops Stortford	78	76	75	77	306
Ted Ray, Ganton	76	77	74	81	308
W. Smith, Mexico	77	71	80	80	308
J. Robson, West Surrey	75	80	77	76	308

1911 SANDWICH

Harry Vardon, South Herts	74	74	75	80	303
Arnaud Massy, St Jean de Luz	75	78	74	76	303
(Play-off; Massy conceded at the 35th hole)					

* Harold Hilton, Royal Liverpool	76	74	78	76	304
Sandy Herd, Coombe Hill	77	73	76	78	304
Ted Ray, Ganton	76	72	79	78	305
James Braid, Walton Heath	78	75	74	78	305
J.H. Taylor, Mid-Surrey	72	76	78	79	305

1912 MUIRFIELD

Ted Ray, Oxhey	71	73	76	75	295
Harry Vardon, South Herts	75	72	81	71	299
James Braid, Walton Heath	77	71	77	78	303
George Duncan, Hanger Hill	72	77	78	78	305
Laurie Ayton, Bishops Stortford	74	80	75	79	308

1913 HOYLAKE

J.H. Taylor, Mid-Surrey	73	75	77	79	304
Ted Ray, Oxhey	73	74	81	84	312
Harry Vardon, South Herts	79	75	79	80	313
M. Moran, Dollymount	76	74	89	74	313
Johnny J. McDermott, USA	75	80	77	83	315
T.G. Renouf, Manchester	75	78	84	78	315

1914 PRESTWICK

Harry Vardon, South Herts	73	77	78	78	306
J.H. Taylor, Mid-Surrey	74	78	74	83	309
H.B. Simpson, St Annes Old	77	80	78	75	310
Abe Mitchell, Sonning	76	78	79	79	312
Tom Williamson, Notts	75	79	79	79	312

1920 DEAL

George Duncan, Hanger Hill	80	80	71	72	303
Sandy Herd, Coombe Hill	72	81	77	75	305
Ted Ray, Oxhey	72	83	78	73	306
Abe Mitchell, North Foreland	74	73	84	76	307
Len Holland, Northampton	80	78	71	79	308
Jim Barnes, USA	79	74	77	79	309

1921 ST ANDREWS

Jock Hutchison, USA	72	75	79	70	296
* Roger Wethered, Royal and Ancient	78	75	72	71	296
(Hutchison won play-off 150 to 159)					
T. Kerrigan, USA	74	80	72	72	298
Arthur G. Havers, West Lancs	76	74	77	72	299
George Duncan, Hanger Hill	74	75	78	74	301

1922 SANDWICH

Walter Hagen, USA	76	73	79	72	300
George Duncan, Hangar Hill	76	75	81	69	301
Jim Barnes, USA	75	76	77	73	301
Jock Hutchison, USA	79	74	73	76	302
Charles Whitcombe, Dorchester	77	79	72	75	303
J.H. Taylor, Mid-Surrey	73	78	76	77	304

1923 TROON

Arthur G. Havers, Coombe Hill	73	73	73	76	295
Walter Hagen, USA	76	71	74	75	296
Macdonald Smith, USA	80	73	69	75	297
Joe Kirkwood, Australia	72	79	69	78	298
Tom Fernie, Turnberry	73	78	74	75	300

1924 HOYLAKE

Walter Hagen, USA	77	73	74	77	301
Ernest Whitcombe, Came Down	77	70	77	78	302
Macdonald Smith, USA	76	74	77	77	304
F. Ball, Langley Park	78	75	74	77	304
J.H. Taylor, Mid-Surrey	75	74	79	79	307

1925 PRESTWICK

Jim Barnes, USA	70	77	79	74	300
Archie Compston, North Manchester	76	75	75	75	301
Ted Ray, Oxhey	77	76	75	73	301
Macdonald Smith, USA	76	69	76	82	303
Abe Mitchell, Unattached	77	76	75	77	305

1926 ROYAL LYTHAM

* Robert T. Jones Jr, USA	72	72	73	74	291
Al Watrous, USA	71	75	69	78	293
Walter Hagen, USA	68	77	74	76	295
George von Elm, USA	75	72	76	72	295
Abe Mitchell, Unattached	78	78	72	71	299
T. Barber, Cavendish	77	73	78	71	299

1927 ST ANDREWS

* Robert T. Jones Jr, USA	68	72	73	72	285
Aubrey Boomer, St Cloud, Paris	76	70	73	72	291
Fred Robson, Cooden Beach	76	72	69	74	291
Joe Kirkwood, Australia	72	72	75	74	293
Ernest Whitcombe, Bournemouth	74	73	73	73	293

1928 SANDWICH

Walter Hagen, USA	75	73	72	72	292
Gene Sarazen, USA	72	76	73	73	294
Archie Compston, Unattached	75	74	73	73	295
Percy Alliss, Berlin	75	76	75	72	298
Fred Robson, Cooden Beach	79	73	73	73	298
Jose Jurado, Argentina	74	71	76	80	301
Aubrey Boomer, St Cloud, Paris	79	73	77	72	301
Jim Barnes, USA	81	73	76	71	301

1929 MUIRFIELD

Walter Hagen, USA	75	67	75	75	292
John Farrell, USA	72	75	76	75	298
Leo Diegel, USA	71	69	82	77	299
Abe Mitchell, St Albans	72	72	78	78	300
Percy Alliss, Berlin	69	76	76	79	300

1930 HOYLAKE

* Robert T. Jones Jr, USA	70	72	74	75	291
Leo Diegel, USA	74	73	71	75	293
Macdonald Smith, USA	70	77	75	71	293
Fred Robson, Cooden Beach	71	72	78	75	296
Horton Smith, USA	72	73	78	73	296
Archie Compston, Coombe Hill	74	73	68	82	297
Jim Barnes, USA	71	77	72	77	297

1931 CARNOUSTIE

Tommy Armour, USA	73	75	77	71	296
Jose Jurado, Argentina	76	71	73	77	297
Percy Alliss, Berlin	74	78	73	73	298
Gene Sarazen, USA	74	76	75	73	298
Macdonald Smith, USA	75	77	71	76	299
John Farrell, USA	72	77	75	75	299

1932 PRINCE'S

Gene Sarazen, USA	70	69	70	74	283
Macdonald Smith, USA	71	76	71	70	288
Arthur G. Havers, Sandy Lodge	74	71	68	76	289
Charles Whitcombe, Crews Hill	71	73	73	75	292
Percy Alliss, Beaconsfield	71	71	78	72	292
Alf Padgham, Royal Ashdown Forest	76	72	74	70	292

1933 ST ANDREWS

Densmore Shute, USA	73	73	73	73	292
Craig Wood, USA	77	72	68	75	292
(Shute won play-off 149 to 154)					
Sid Easterbrook, Knowle	73	72	71	77	293
Gene Sarazen, USA	72	73	73	75	293
Leo Diegel, USA	75	70	71	77	293

1934 SANDWICH

Henry Cotton, Waterloo, Belgium	67	65	72	79	283
Sid Brews, South Africa	76	71	70	71	288
Alf Padgham, Sundridge Park	71	70	75	74	290
Macdonald Smith, USA	77	71	72	72	292
Joe Kirkwood, USA	74	69	71	78	292
Marcel Dallemagne, France	71	73	71	77	292

1935 MUIRFIELD

Alf Perry, Leatherhead	69	75	67	72	283
Alf Padgham, Sundridge Park	70	72	74	71	287
Charles Whitcombe, Crews Hill	71	68	73	76	288
Bert Gadd, Brand Hall	72	75	71	71	289
Lawson Little, USA	75	71	74	69	289

1936 HOYLAKE

Alf Padgham, Sundridge Park	73	72	71	71	287
Jimmy Adams, Romford	71	73	71	73	288
Henry Cotton, Waterloo, Belgium	73	72	70	74	289
Marcel Dallemagne, France	73	72	75	69	289
Percy Alliss, Leeds Municipal	74	72	74	71	291
T. Green, Burnham Beeches	74	72	70	75	291
Gene Sarazen, USA	73	75	70	73	291

1937 CARNOUSTIE

Henry Cotton, Ashridge	74	72	73	71	290
Reg Whitcombe, Parkstone	72	70	74	76	292
Charles Lacey, USA	76	75	70	72	293
Charles Whitcombe, Crews Hill	73	71	74	76	294
Bryon Nelson, USA	75	76	71	74	296

1938 SANDWICH

Reg Whitcombe, Parkstone	71	71	75	78	295
Jimmy Adams, Royal Liverpool	70	71	78	78	297
Henry Cotton, Ashridge	74	73	77	74	298
Alf Padgham, Sundridge Park	74	72	75	82	303
Jack Busson, Pannal	71	69	83	80	303
Richard Burton, Sale	71	69	78	85	303
Allan Dailey, Wanstead	73	72	80	78	303

1939 ST ANDREWS

Richard Burton, Sale	70	72	77	71	290
Johnny Bulla, USA	77	71	71	73	292
Johnny Fallon, Huddersfield	71	73	71	79	294
Bill Shankland, Temple Newsam	72	73	72	77	294
Alf Perry, Leatherhead	71	74	73	76	294
Reg Whitcombe, Parkstone	71	75	74	74	294
Sam King, Knole Park	74	72	75	73	294

1946 ST ANDREWS

Sam Snead, USA	71	70	74	75	290
Bobby Locke, South Africa	69	74	75	76	294
Johnny Bulla, USA	71	72	72	79	294
Charlie Ward, Little Aston	73	73	73	76	295
Henry Cotton, Royal Mid-Surrey	70	70	76	79	295
Dai Rees, Hindhead	75	67	73	80	295
Norman von Nida, Australia	70	76	74	75	295

1947 HOYLAKE

Fred Daly, Balmoral, Belfast	73	70	78	72	293
Reg Horne, Hendon	77	74	72	71	294
* Frank Stranahan, USA	71	79	72	72	294
Bill Shankland, Temple Newsam	76	74	75	70	295
Richard Burton, Coombe Hill	77	71	77	71	296
Charlie Ward, Little Aston	76	73	76	72	297
Sam King, Wildernesse	75	72	77	73	297
Arthur Lees, Dore and Totley	75	74	72	76	297
Johnny Bulla, USA	80	72	74	71	297
Henry Cotton, Royal Mid-Surrey	69	78	74	76	297
Norman von Nida, Australia	74	76	71	76	297

1948 MUIRFIELD

Henry Cotton, Royal Mid-Surrey	71	66	75	72	284
Fred Daly, Balmoral, Belfast	72	71	73	73	289
Norman von Nida, Australia	71	72	76	71	290
Roberto de Vicenzo, Argentina	70	73	72	75	290
Jack Hargreaves, Sutton Coldfield	76	68	73	73	290
Charlie Ward, Little Aston	69	72	75	74	290

1949 SANDWICH

Bobby Locke, South Africa	69	76	68	70	283
Harry Bradshaw, Kilcroney, Eire	68	77	68	70	283
(Locke won play-off 135 to 147)					
Roberto de Vicenzo, Argentina	68	75	73	69	285
Sam King, Knole Park	71	69	74	72	286
Charlie Ward, Little Aston	73	71	70	72	286
Arthur Lees, Dore and Totley	74	70	72	71	287
Max Faulkner, Royal Mid-Surrey	71	71	71	74	287

1950 TROON

Bobby Locke, South Africa	69	72	70	68	279
Roberto de Vicenzo, Argentina	72	71	68	70	281
Fred Daly, Balmoral, Belfast	75	72	69	66	282
Dai Rees, South Herts	71	68	72	71	282
E. Moore, South Africa	74	68	73	68	283
Max Faulkner, Royal Mid-Surrey	73	70	70	71	283

1951 ROYAL PORTRUSH

Max Faulkner, Unattached	71	70	70	74	285
Tony Cerda, Argentina	74	72	71	70	287
Charlie Ward, Little Aston	75	73	74	68	290
Fred Daly, Balmoral, Belfast	74	70	75	73	292
Jimmy Adams, Wentworth	68	77	75	72	292
Bobby Locke, South Africa	71	74	74	74	293
Bill Shankland, Temple Newsam	73	76	72	72	293
Norman Sutton, Leigh	73	70	74	76	293
Harry Weetman, Croham Hurst	73	71	75	74	293
Peter Thomson, Australia	70	75	73	75	293

1952 ROYAL LYTHAM

Bobby Locke, South Africa	69	71	74	73	287
Peter Thomson, Australia	68	73	77	70	288
Fred Daly, Balmoral, Belfast	67	69	77	76	289
Henry Cotton, Royal Mid-Surrey	75	74	74	71	294
Tony Cerda, Argentina	73	73	76	73	295
Sam King, Knole Park	71	74	74	76	295

1953 CARNOUSTIE

Ben Hogan, USA	73	71	70	68	282
* Frank Stranahan, USA	70	74	73	69	286
Dai Rees, South Herts	72	70	73	71	286
Peter Thomson, Australia	72	72	71	71	286
Tony Cerda, Argentina	75	71	69	71	286
Roberto de Vicenzo, Argentina	72	71	71	73	287

1954 ROYAL BIRKDALE

Peter Thomson, Australia	72	71	69	71	283
Sid Scott, Carlisle City	76	67	69	72	284
Dai Rees, South Herts	72	71	69	72	284
Bobby Locke, South Africa	74	71	69	70	284
Jimmy Adams, Royal Mid-Surrey	73	75	69	69	286
Tony Cerda, Argentina	71	71	73	71	286
J. Turnesa, USA	72	72	71	71	286

1955 ST ANDREWS

Peter Thomson, Australia	71	68	70	72	281
Johnny Fallon, Huddersfield	73	67	73	70	283
Frank Jowle, Edgbaston	70	71	69	74	284
Bobby Locke, South Africa	74	69	70	72	285
Tony Cerda, Argentina	73	71	71	71	286
Ken Bousfield, Coombe Hill	71	75	70	70	286
Harry Weetman, Croham Hurst	71	71	70	74	286
Bernard Hunt, Hartsbourne	70	71	74	71	286
Flory van Donck, Belgium	71	72	71	72	286

1956 HOYLAKE

Peter Thomson, Australia	70	70	72	74	286
Flory van Donck, Belgium	71	74	70	74	289
Roberto de Vicenzo, Argentina	71	70	79	70	290
Gary Player, South Africa	71	76	73	71	291
John Panton, Glenbervie	74	76	72	70	292
Henry Cotton, Temple	72	76	71	74	293
E. Bertolino, Argentina	69	72	76	76	293

1957 ST ANDREWS

Bobby Locke, South Africa	69	72	68	70	279
Peter Thomson, Australia	73	69	70	70	282
Eric Brown, Buchanan Castle	67	72	73	71	283
Angel Miguel, Spain	72	72	69	72	285
David Thomas, Sudbury	72	74	70	70	286
Tom Haliburton, Wentworth	72	73	68	73	286
* Dick Smith, Prestwick	71	72	72	71	286
Flory van Donck, Belgium	72	68	74	72	286

1958 ROYAL LYTHAM

Peter Thomson, Australia	66	72	67	73	278
David Thomas, Sudbury	70	68	69	71	278
(Thomson won play-off 139 to 143)					
Eric Brown, Buchanan Castle	73	70	65	71	279
Christy O'Connor, Killarney	67	68	73	71	279
Flory van Donck, Belgium	70	70	67	74	281
Leopoldo Ruiz, Argentina	71	65	72	73	281

1959 MUIRFIELD

Gary Player, South Africa	75	71	70	68	284
Flory van Donck, Belgium	70	70	73	73	286
Fred Bullock, Prestwick St Ninians	68	70	74	74	286
Sid Scott, Roehampton	73	70	73	71	287
Christy O'Connor, Royal Dublin	73	74	72	69	288
* Reid Jack, Dullatur	71	75	68	74	288
Sam King, Knole Park	70	74	68	76	288
John Panton, Glenbervie	72	72	71	73	288

1960 ST ANDREWS

Kel Nagle, Australia	69	67	71	71	278
Arnold Palmer, USA	70	71	70	68	279
Bernard Hunt, Hartsbourne	72	73	71	66	282
Harold Henning, South Africa	72	72	69	69	282
Roberto de Vicenzo, Argentina	67	67	75	73	282

1961 ROYAL BIRKDALE

Arnold Palmer, USA	70	73	69	72	284
Dai Rees, South Herts	68	74	71	72	285
Christy O'Connor, Royal Dublin	71	77	67	73	288
Neil Coles, Coombe Hill	70	77	69	72	288
Eric Brown, Unattached	73	76	70	70	289
Kel Nagle, Australia	68	75	75	71	289

1962 TROON

Arnold Palmer, USA	71	69	67	69	276
Kel Nagle, Australia	71	71	70	70	282
Brian Huggett, Romford	75	71	74	69	289
Phil Rodgers, USA	75	70	72	72	289
Bob Charles, NZ	75	70	70	75	290
Sam Snead, USA	76	73	72	71	292
Peter Thomson, Australia	70	77	75	70	292

1963 ROYAL LYTHAM

Bob Charles, NZ	68	72	66	71	277
Phil Rodgers, USA	67	68	73	69	277
(Charles won play-off 140 to 148)					
Jack Nicklaus, USA	71	67	70	70	278
Kel Nagle, Australia	69	70	73	71	283
Peter Thomson, Australia	67	69	71	78	285

1964 ST ANDREWS

Tony Lema, USA	73	68	68	70	279
Jack Nicklaus, USA	76	74	66	68	284
Roberto de Vicenzo, Argentina	76	72	70	67	285
Bernard Hunt, Hartsbourne	73	74	70	70	287
Bruce Devlin, Australia	72	72	73	73	290

1965 ROYAL BIRKDALE

Peter Thomson, Australia	74	68	72	71	285
Christy O'Connor, Royal Dublin	69	73	74	71	287
Brian Huggett, Romford	73	68	76	70	287
Roberto de Vicenzo, Argentina	74	69	73	72	288
Kel Nagle, Australia	74	70	73	72	289
Tony Lema, USA	68	72	75	74	289
Bernard Hunt, Hartsbourne	74	74	70	71	289

1966 MUIRFIELD

Jack Nicklaus, USA	70	67	75	70	282
David Thomas, Dunham Forest	72	73	69	69	283
Doug Sanders, USA	71	70	72	70	283
Gary Player, South Africa	72	74	71	69	286
Bruce Devlin, Australia	73	69	74	70	286
Kel Nagle, Australia	72	68	76	70	286
Phil Rodgers, USA	74	66	70	76	286

1967 HOYLAKE

Roberto de Vicenzo, Argentina	70	71	67	70	278
Jack Nicklaus, USA	71	69	71	69	280
Clive Clark, Sunningdale	70	73	69	72	284
Gary Player, South Africa	72	71	67	74	284
Tony Jacklin, Potters Bar	73	69	73	70	285

1968 CARNOUSTIE

Gary Player, South Africa	74	71	71	73	289
Jack Nicklaus, USA	76	69	73	73	291
Bob Charles, NZ	72	72	71	76	291
Billy Casper, USA	72	68	74	78	292
Maurice Bembridge, Little Aston	71	75	73	74	293

1969 ROYAL LYTHAM

Tony Jacklin, Potters Bar	68	70	70	72	280
Bob Charles, NZ	66	69	75	72	282
Peter Thomson, Australia	71	70	70	72	283
Roberto de Vicenzo, Argentina	72	73	66	72	283
Christy O'Connor, Royal Dublin	71	65	74	74	284
Jack Nicklaus, USA	75	70	68	72	285
Davis Love Jr, USA	70	73	71	71	285

1970 ST ANDREWS

Jack Nicklaus, USA	68	69	73	73	283
Doug Sanders, USA	68	71	71	73	283
(Nicklaus won play-off 72 to 73)					
Harold Henning, South Africa	67	72	73	73	285
Lee Trevino, USA	68	68	72	77	285
Tony Jacklin, Potters Bar	67	70	73	76	286

1971 ROYAL BIRKDALE

Lee Trevino, USA	69	70	69	70	278
Lu Liang Huan, Taiwan	70	70	69	70	279
Tony Jacklin, Potters Bar	69	70	70	71	280
Craig de Foy, Coombe Hill	72	72	68	69	281
Jack Nicklaus, USA	71	71	72	69	283
Charles Coody, USA	74	71	70	68	283

1972 MUIRFIELD

Lee Trevino, USA	71	70	66	71	278
Jack Nicklaus, USA	70	72	71	66	279
Tony Jacklin, Potters Bar	69	72	67	72	280
Doug Sanders, USA	71	71	69	70	281
Brian Barnes, Fairway DR	71	72	69	71	283
Gary Player, South Africa	71	71	76	67	285

1973 TROON

Tom Weiskopf, USA	68	67	71	70	276
Neil Coles, Holiday Inns	71	72	70	66	279
Johnny Miller, USA	70	68	69	72	279
Jack Nicklaus, USA	69	70	76	65	280
Bert Yancey, USA	69	69	73	70	281

1974 ROYAL LYTHAM

Gary Player, South Africa	69	68	75	70	282
Peter Oosterhuis, Pacific Harbour	71	71	73	71	286
Jack Nicklaus, USA	74	72	70	71	287
Hubert Green, USA	71	74	72	71	288
Danny Edwards, USA	70	73	76	73	292
Lu Liang Huan, Taiwan	72	72	75	73	292

1975 CARNOUSTIE

Tom Watson, USA	71	67	69	72	279
Jack Newton, Australia	69	71	65	74	279
(Watson won play-off 71 to 72)					
Bobby Cole, South Africa	72	66	66	76	280
Jack Nicklaus, USA	69	71	68	72	280
Johnny Miller, USA	71	69	66	74	280

1976 ROYAL BIRKDALE

Johnny Miller, USA	72	68	73	66	279
Jack Nicklaus, USA	74	70	72	69	285
Severiano Ballesteros, Spain	69	69	73	74	285
Raymond Floyd, USA	76	67	73	70	286
Mark James, Burghley Park	76	72	74	66	288
Hubert Green, USA	72	70	78	68	288
Christy O'Connor Jr, Shannon	69	73	75	71	288
Tom Kite, USA	70	74	73	71	288
Tommy Horton, Royal Jersey	74	69	72	73	288

1977 TURNBERRY

Tom Watson, USA	68	70	65	65	268
Jack Nicklaus, USA	68	70	65	66	269
Hubert Green, USA	72	66	74	67	279
Lee Trevino, USA	68	70	72	70	280
Ben Crenshaw, USA	71	69	66	75	281
George Burns, USA	70	70	72	69	281

1978 ST ANDREWS

Jack Nicklaus, USA	71	72	69	69	281
Simon Owen, NZ	70	75	67	71	283
Ben Crenshaw, USA	70	69	73	71	283
Raymond Floyd, USA	69	75	71	68	283
Tom Kite, USA	72	69	72	70	283

1979 ROYAL LYTHAM

Severiano Ballesteros, Spain	73	65	75	70	283
Jack Nicklaus, USA	72	69	73	72	286
Ben Crenshaw, USA	72	71	72	71	286
Mark James, Burghley Park	76	69	69	73	287
Rodger Davis, Australia	75	70	70	73	288

1980 MUIRFIELD

Tom Watson, USA	68	70	64	69	271
Lee Trevino, USA	68	67	71	69	275
Ben Crenshaw, USA	70	70	68	69	277
Jack Nicklaus, USA	73	67	71	69	280
Carl Mason, Unattached	72	69	70	69	280

1981 SANDWICH

Bill Rogers, USA	72	66	67	71	276
Bernhard Langer, Germany	73	67	70	70	280
Mark James, Otley	72	70	68	73	283
Raymond Floyd, USA	74	70	69	70	283
Sam Torrance, Caledonian Hotel	72	69	73	70	284

1982 TROON

Tom Watson, USA	69	71	74	70	284
Peter Oosterhuis, GB	74	67	74	70	285
Nick Price, South Africa	69	69	74	73	285
Nick Faldo, Glynwed Ltd	73	73	71	69	286
Des Smyth, EAL Tubes	70	69	74	73	286
Tom Purtzer, USA	76	66	75	69	286
Massy Kuramoto, Japan	71	73	71	71	286

1983 ROYAL BIRKDALE

Tom Watson, USA	67	68	70	70	275
Hale Irwin, USA	69	68	72	67	276
Andy Bean, USA	70	69	70	67	276
Graham Marsh, Australia	69	70	74	64	277
Lee Trevino, USA	69	66	73	70	278
Severiano Ballesteros, Spain	71	71	69	68	279
Harold Henning, South Africa	71	69	70	69	279

1984 ST ANDREWS

Severiano Ballesteros, Spain	69	68	70	69	276
Bernhard Langer, Germany	71	68	68	71	278
Tom Watson, USA	71	68	66	73	278
Fred Couples, USA	70	69	74	68	281
Lanny Wadkins, USA	70	69	73	69	281
Greg Norman, Australia	67	74	74	67	282
Nick Faldo, Glynwed Int.	69	68	76	69	282

1985 SANDWICH

Sandy Lyle, Scotland	68	71	73	70	282
Payne Stewart, USA	70	75	70	68	283
Jose Rivero, Spain	74	72	70	68	284
Christy O'Connor Jr, Ireland	64	76	72	72	284
Mark O'Meara, USA	70	72	70	72	284
David Graham, Australia	68	71	70	75	284
Bernhard Langer, Germany	72	69	68	75	284

1986 TURNBERRY

Greg Norman, Australia	74	63	74	69	280
Gordon J. Brand, England	71	68	75	71	285
Bernhard Langer, Germany	72	70	76	68	286
Ian Woosnam, Wales	70	74	70	72	286
Nick Faldo, England	71	70	76	70	287

1987 MUIRFIELD

Nick Faldo, England	68	69	71	71	279
Rodger Davis, Australia	64	73	74	69	280
Paul Azinger, USA	68	68	71	73	280
Ben Crenshaw, USA	73	68	72	68	281
Payne Stewart, USA	71	66	72	72	281

1988 ROYAL LYTHAM

Severiano Ballesteros, Spain	67	71	70	65	273
Nick Price, Zimbabwe	70	67	69	69	275
Nick Faldo, England	71	69	68	71	279
Fred Couples, USA	73	69	71	68	281
Gary Koch, USA	71	72	70	68	281

1989 ROYAL TROON

Mark Calcavecchia, USA	71	68	68	68	275
Greg Norman, Australia	69	70	72	64	275
Wayne Grady, Australia	68	67	69	71	275
(Calcavecchia won four-hole play-off)					
Tom Watson, USA	69	68	68	72	277
Jodie Mudd, USA	73	67	68	70	278

1990 ST ANDREWS

Nick Faldo, England	67	65	67	71	270
Mark McNulty, Zimbabwe	74	68	68	65	275
Payne Stewart, USA	68	68	68	71	275
Jodie Mudd, USA	72	66	72	66	276
Ian Woosnam, Wales	68	69	70	69	276

1991 ROYAL BIRKDALE

Ian Baker-Finch, Australia	71	71	64	66	272
Mike Harwood, Australia	68	70	69	67	274
Fred Couples, USA	72	69	70	64	275
Mark O'Meara, USA	71	68	67	69	275
Jodie Mudd, USA	72	70	72	63	277
Bob Tway, USA	75	66	70	66	277
Eamonn Darcy, Ireland	73	68	66	70	277

1992 MUIRFIELD

Nick Faldo, England	66	64	69	73	272
John Cook, USA	66	67	70	70	273
Jose Maria Olazabal, Spain	70	67	69	68	274
Steve Pate, USA	64	70	69	73	276
Andrew Magee, USA	67	72	70	70	279
Malcolm Mackenzie, England	71	67	70	71	279
Robert Karlsson, Sweden	70	68	70	71	279
Ian Woosnam, Wales	65	73	70	71	279
Gordon Brand Jr, Scotland	65	68	72	74	279
Donnie Hammond, USA	70	65	70	74	279
Ernie Els, South Africa	66	69	70	74	279

1993 SANDWICH

Greg Norman, Australia	66	68	69	64	267
Nick Faldo, England	69	63	70	67	269
Bernhard Langer, Germany	67	66	70	67	270
Peter Senior, Australia	66	69	70	67	272
Corey Pavin, USA	68	66	68	70	272

FINAL RESULTS

HOLE		1	2	3	4	5	6	7	8	9	10	11	12	13	14	15	16	17	18	
PAR		4	4	4	3	4	3	5	4	4	4	3	4	4	4	3	4	5	4	TOTAL
Nick Price	Round 1	4	3	3	3	5	3	4	4	4	4	3	5	4	4	3	4	5	4	69
	Round 2	3	4	3	4	4	2	4	5	4	4	3	4	3	4	3	3	4	5	66
	Round 3	4	3	4	3	4	3	4	4	4	4	3	4	4	4	2	4	4	5	67
	Round 4	4	5	4	2	5	3	4	4	4	4	3	3	4	4	3	3	3	4	66-268
Jesper Parnevik	Round 1	4	4	5	3	3	3	4	4	4	4	2	5	4	4	2	4	5	4	68
	Round 2	4	4	4	2	4	4	3	5	4	4	3	4	4	4	2	3	4	4	67
	Round 3	4	4	4	3	5	4	4	4	4	3	3	3	5	4	3	3	4	4	68
	Round 4	4	4	4	3	4	3	5	4	4	4	2	3	3	4	4	3	4	5	67-269
Fuzzy Zoeller	Round 1	4	4	4	4	3	3	5	4	5	3	3	5	4	4	3	4	4	5	71
	Round 2	4	4	4	2	5	2	4	4	4	4	2	4	5	4	2	4	4	4	66
	Round 3	3	4	4	3	5	2	4	4	4	4	3	3	3	4	3	3	4	4	64
	Round 4	4	3	4	3	4	4	5	4	5	4	2	4	5	4	3	4	5	3	70-271
Anders Forsbrand	Round 1	4	4	4	3	5	3	3	5	4	4	3	5	5	4	3	4	5	4	72
	Round 2	3	5	4	3	5	3	5	5	4	4	3	4	5	5	3	3	4	3	71
	Round 3	3	4	4	3	3	3	5	3	4	4	3	4	4	5	3	4	4	3	66
	Round 4	4	4	4	2	4	3	5	4	3	3	2	4	4	4	3	4	3	4	64-273
Mark James	Round 1	4	4	4	3	5	4	4	4	3	4	3	6	4	5	2	3	5	5	72
	Round 2	4	4	4	3	4	3	5	5	4	4	2	4	4	4	3	3	4	3	67
	Round 3	4	4	4	3	4	3	4	3	5	4	3	3	3	4	2	4	5	4	66
	Round 4	4	4	4	2	4	4	5	4	4	4	3	4	4	6	2	4	3	3	68-273
David Feherty	Round 1	4	5	4	2	4	2	4	4	4	3	3	4	5	4	3	4	4	5	68
	Round 2	4	4	4	2	4	3	4	4	4	4	3	5	4	4	4	4	4	4	69
	Round 3	4	4	4	3	3	3	5	4	4	3	3	4	4	4	2	4	4	4	66
	Round 4	4	4	4	3	4	3	5	4	4	3	3	4	4	4	3	4	6	4	70-273
Brad Faxon	Round 1	4	4	4	3	4	3	4	5	4	3	3	5	5	4	2	4	4	4	69
	Round 2	4	4	4	2	4	3	4	4	3	4	3	4	4	4	2	4	4	4	65
	Round 3	4	3	4	3	4	3	5	4	4	3	3	4	4	4	3	4	4	4	67
	Round 4	5	4	4	3	4	4	5	4	4	5	3	4	4	4	3	4	5	4	73-274
Nick Faldo	Round 1	4	4	5	3	4	3	5	5	4	4	3	4	4	4	3	4	8	4	75
	Round 2	4	4	4	3	4	3	5	3	4	4	2	4	4	4	3	4	4	3	66
	Round 3	4	4	4	3	5	3	5	4	4	5	3	3	4	4	3	3	4	5	70
	Round 4	3	4	5	3	4	2	3	4	4	3	3	4	4	4	3	3	4	4	64-275
Tom Kite	Round 1	5	4	5	3	4	4	4	4	3	3	3	4	5	3	3	5	5	4	71
	Round 2	5	4	4	2	4	3	5	3	4	4	3	4	4	4	4	4	4	4	69
	Round 3	3	4	4	4	4	3	5	4	4	4	4	3	3	3	3	4	3	4	66
	Round 4	3	3	4	2	4	3	5	5	5	5	2	4	4	4	3	3	4	6	69-275
Colin Montgomerie	Round 1	4	4	4	3	4	3	4	5	4	4	3	5	4	4	3	5	5	4	72
	Round 2	4	4	4	2	3	4	5	4	6	4	3	5	3	5	3	3	4	3	69
	Round 3	3	4	4	2	5	3	4	5	3	3	3	4	4	4	3	3	5	3	65
	Round 4	4	4	4	3	4	3	5	4	4	4	2	5	3	4	3	4	5	4	69-275